A CUP OF COMFORT®
Book of
Prayer

Stories and reflections
that bring you
closer to God

Edited by James Stuart Bell
& Susan B. Townsend

Aadamsmedia
Avon, Massachusetts

To Brigit Bell Ritchie and Susie Burgess—
prayer warriors entering motherhood—JB

Dedicated to my mother, Barbara Clark Armstrong, who taught me to pray.
And to Thomas E.—living proof that God wants me to be happy.—ST

Copyright © 2007 by F+W Publications, Inc.
All rights reserved. This book, or parts thereof, may not be
reproduced in any form without permission from the publisher;
exceptions are made for brief excerpts used in published reviews.

A Cup of Comfort® is a registered trademark of F+W Publications, Inc.

Published by
Adams Media, an F+W Publications Company
57 Littlefield Street, Avon, MA 02322. U.S.A.
www.adamsmedia.com and *www.cupofcomfort.com*

ISBN-10: 1-59869-345-X
ISBN-13: 978-1-59869-345-4

Printed in the United States of America.

J I H G F E D C B A

Library of Congress Cataloging-in-Publication Data
A cup of comfort book of prayer / edited by James Stuart Bell
and Susan B. Townsend.
p.   cm. — (A cup of comfort book.)
ISBN-13: 978-1-59869-345-4 (pbk.)
ISBN-10: 1-59869-345-X (pbk.)
1. Prayer—Christianity. 2. Spiritual life—Christianity.
3. Christian life—Anecdotes. 4. Prayers. I. Bell, James Stuart.
II. Townsend, Susan
BV210.3.C87 2007
248.3'2—dc22   2007017703

Unless otherwise noted, the Bible used as a source is *Holy Bible: New Living
Translation*, Tyndale House Publishers.

This book is available at quantity discounts for bulk purchases.
For information, please call 1-800-289-0963.

Contents

Introduction

Over the centuries Christian books, manuals, and guides of all sorts have been written to help us understand the nature of prayer and to pray more effectively. Some stress the profound and mystical depths of prayer and even union with God. Others discuss the practical aspects of prayer in our everyday life.

Actually, prayer at its basic level is very simple. God has made a way for us through Jesus to come to Him just as we are, with all our faults, problems, and needs. We don't need to earn our way into His presence or be filled with pious language. We worship Him certainly because of all His greatness and perfection found in Scripture and knowing His unsurpassable love shown us in the life and death of Jesus. But we can also be completely honest about our fears, disappointments, and pain. As we look at His promises in Scripture regarding prayer, we can be encouraged and comforted, confident that He will answer in His own way and own time.

Those answers become apparent as you talk to Christians who take prayer seriously. Some of God's answers are subtle and some are miraculous. Some relate to something as simple as a changed attitude, whereas others point to physical healing that goes beyond a doctor's explanation. What becomes evident is that God is active and interested in the smallest details of our lives. For some reason known only to Him, certain circumstances require our asking, thanking, and worshipping Him to bring about the positive change that He and we so greatly desire.

Stories in which prayer is the catalyst for the positive transformation of our lives are full of surprises and wonder. They motivate us to approach God's "throne of grace" with boldness as we see His power and love graphically demonstrated in the lives of others. That is the main purpose of this collection of stories, in which prayer plays a pivotal role.

Each story is accompanied by a prayer that is relevant to its content. Similar to those found in books of prayer compilations, you can use these prayers as they relate to issues in your own life. You may even want to create a notebook including your favorites from this volume and use it throughout the day.

~James Stuart Bell and Susan B. Townsend

Acknowledgments

We acknowledge, as always, the editors who excel in the genre of storytelling and provide the guidance so necessary—Paula Munier and Brendan O'Neill. And Gary Krebs, who provides the overall leadership and vision.

As editors we thank this volume's contributors for sharing their powerful examples of God being there for them when they needed Him most. We pray that He will be there for you too, to provide for all your needs and bring you great joy as you explore His fathomless depths through the privilege of prayer that is His gift to us.

Ramp of Hope

*. . . Father, the hour has come. Glorify
your Son so he can give glory back to you.
For you have given him authority over
everyone. He gives eternal life to each one
you have given him. And this is the way to
have eternal life—to know you, the only
true God, and Jesus Christ, the one you
sent to earth. I brought glory to you here
on earth by completing the work you gave
me to do. Now, Father, bring me into the
glory we shared before the world began.*

—John 17:1–5

When we entered the gymnasium at 10:30
P.M., we found things had already settled
down for the night. We were instructed by an older
woman to pull an air mattress from a lofty stack hidden in a far corner of the room. Burdened with our
bed for the next week, we carefully maneuvered our
way through seemingly lifeless bodies spread across
the floor like small fortresses. Our only guidance was

the occasional snore that erupted from a sleeping bag here and there. We pushed through the shadows, attempting to find an empty spot on the floor where we, too, could build our own little fortress. We tripped over suitcases and blow dryers at every step. Eventually, we found a space, dropped our bags, and took a deep breath while our eyes adjusted to the darkness.

That was when I started to wonder what I'd gotten myself into. I had ridden in a van full of people for more than 900 miles, only to find our greeters dead to the world. I had come with a purpose, and I wanted to make a difference. I was ready to change the life of a victim of the Hurricane Katrina tragedy. Why was everyone asleep? I wanted to shout, "C'mon people—let's go!"

Our group of twenty had traveled from Spring Hill, Kansas, to Gautier, Mississippi, to a local church that generously opened their brand-new building to house the Work and Witness groups who came to volunteer. Not only did they open their gymnasium, but they also provided breakfast in the morning, sack lunches at noon, and a warm meal in the evening. There were even showers available after a long day of hard work, although the hot water was on a first come, first served basis.

When morning started creeping through the

small cracks under the gymnasium doors, people made their way to the kitchen for breakfast prepared by volunteers. After everyone had eaten, there was a devotional, then a short meeting led by two or three men who had been sleeping on those hard wooden floors for months and going out every day to the endless job of cleaning up. They welcomed the newcomers, discussed the schedule for the day, and assigned the groups to specific job sites. Our team soon had a plan. We grabbed our sack lunches and set off to what we would discover was an interminable job of cleaning up, filth, and heartache.

Since we had come in late the night before, it wasn't until that morning that the realization of the horrible devastation hit us. Streets once lined with gorgeous trees were empty and bare. Buildings once thriving with business were nothing but hollow shells. The hurricane hit over fifty miles of the Mississippi shoreline, wiping out nearly every home as far as five blocks in from the coast. Beautifully kept beach homes, some handed down through generations, were now piles of debris and rubble.

We saw a staircase standing with nothing to support it. A single stove remained where an entire kitchen had once been. Shoes and toys that children had cherished were scattered and torn into small pieces. The more we looked, the more personal it became. One backyard had debris strewn everywhere, but resting at the side of the family swimming pool stood a single Precious Moments angel statue—upright and completely unscathed.

That day, some of our group went to a local home and began gutting it piece by piece. We wore protective clothing, masks, and gloves, being careful not to breathe in the deadly mold that grew on every section of wood and ruin. Others went to a local church where they hung Sheetrock on new framework.

A young woman saw the workers at the church and stopped to ask if they knew where City Hall had been moved. They told her they were from out of town and didn't know, but they asked her if she needed any work done. Her friendly disposition won them over immediately. Even though she was flustered by her circumstances, she wore a smile that never seemed to fade. It wasn't long until the two groups met up and went to her home, where we learned her story.

Suzanne was a single mom who had lived in the area her entire life. She and her two young daughters were living with her parents in her childhood home. After the disaster nearly destroyed their house, the girls went to live with relatives in another state, and Suzanne's parents moved to a nearby shelter.

All hurricane victims were required to get a tetanus shot. Suzanne's mother received hers at the same time as a flu shot, and because of a possible allergic reaction, she contracted Guillain-Barré syndrome. GBS is a disorder of the peripheral nerves that can sometimes cause paralysis. Suzanne's mother became paralyzed from the waist down, and Suzanne asked our team to come and build a handicap ramp so her parents could return home—to a very small, borrowed travel trailer, parked in the driveway.

Authorities had allowed residents to return to the area, so Suzanne's daughters had come home. Suzanne was looking for City Hall so she could enroll them in school, but her parents couldn't return from the shelter until her mom had a way to get into the trailer.

We worked incredibly hard over the next couple of days. Some of us picked up shards of glass, pieces of torn photos, and small fragments from the yard and cleaned up what was left inside the house, while others built a wheelchair-accessible ramp with rails. It quickly became obvious why the volunteers had been sound asleep at 10:30 P.M. the night we arrived.

Suzanne kept us entertained with stories as we worked, and it wasn't long before we thought of her as an old friend. Soon, the ramp was complete, and it was time to say good-bye. She expressed her gratitude and told us she had been truly blessed by our efforts, but we, too, had felt God's blessing. We had been touched in a way that would change our lives, and we were honored that God used us to glorify Him.

We prayed with Suzanne and the girls, hugged them, and said our good-byes. Before we left, she asked if she could give us something. She took a small frame from her shelf and told us it was one of the few things she had been able to salvage from her home. With tears in our eyes, we read the embroidered words: "Work for the Lord. The pay isn't much, but the retirement plan is out of this world!" We couldn't possibly accept her generous gift, but we did take a photo of her holding it. That picture will be etched in our minds forever!

We have kept in touch with Suzanne. In a recent letter, she wrote that since we were there, people from all over the United States have come to help her family in one way or another. She always asks them to sign the ramp and said the messages touch everyone who reads them. She calls it her "Ramp of Hope"!

One of the ways we serve God while we are on earth is by doing the things He asks of us.

God will disclose His will if we study His word and listen to Him in prayer. We may receive our thanks for a job well done from our friends here on earth, but just like Jesus, we know that all honor and glory belong to God.

~Jennie Hilligus

Burnout

The Lord is my shepherd;
    I have all that I need.
He lets me rest in green meadows;
    he leads me beside peaceful streams.
He renews my strength.
He guides me along right paths,
    bringing honor to his name.
Even when I walk
    through the darkest valley,
I will not be afraid,
    for you are close beside me.
Your rod and your staff
    protect and comfort me.
You prepare a feast for me
    in the presence of my enemies.
You honor me by anointing my head with oil.
    My cup overflows with blessings.
Surely your goodness and unfailing
love will pursue me
    all the days of my life,
and I will live in the house of the Lord
    forever.

—Psalm 23

I left the hospital and walked across the parking lot, the tears freezing on my face. To leave my husband, Leo, in the emergency ward meant trusting him to other hands. I yearned to help, to hold, to have a part in his healing, but God was choosing other people for that avenue of service. Reassured by the presence of two capable doctors at his bedside, I drove home to be with our teenagers.

They were curious, concerned, but careful not to shed any tears for fear of prompting a flood of emotion. Not until I reached the privacy of our bedroom did my own pent-up emotions burst forth. Burying my face in my pillow to stifle the sound of my sobs, I reached for the crumpled tissue Leo had used to wipe his feverish brow just hours before. The symptoms had duped the doctors into treating him for pneumonia, but scans had revealed blood clots on both lungs. After numerous tests, the doctors concluded his condition was stress related. His blood chemistry had apparently reacted negatively to burnout.

Burnout.

I picked up the temperamental alarm clock that works only when lying facedown on the rug. As I turned it over, it stopped at 11:37 P.M. I was sharply aware of the doctor's words that the next seventy-two hours would be critical, that the shadow of death hovered over us. Leo's work clothes lay rolled in a bundle, his belt neatly coiled on the dresser. Church books were just where he had left them on the desk, the ledger open at January 1. Illness was a new experience at the beginning of a new year, and my tendency was to shrink back in fear. But as I looked at the neat rows of figures printed in a firm, strong hand, I was reassured that, whatever lay ahead, the balance of our lives was still within the purpose of God.

As I turned back the blankets, my husband's crooked old slippers peeked out from under the bed. "Those are big shoes to fill," someone in the church family had recently remarked. "It takes love for the Lord's work and lots of enthusiasm," I had replied. Leo's plaid slippers, worn thin from use, yet dearly beloved, seemed somehow symbolic of his involvement, as did his dog-eared Bible bulging with lesson notes, deacon memos, hymn numbers, and Sunday bulletins.

I chose to lie on his side of the bed, cradled by the sense of his presence and strangely comforted. I pondered whether this situation could have been avoided under less stressful conditions, whether we had been negligent in terms of health or simply obedient to what God asked. An observant friend, upon hearing of Leo's condition, likened the situation to the burnout experienced by Epaphroditus, an early church worker, whom the apostle Paul described as

almost dying because he risked his life "to compen-
sate for the deficiency of others."

Apathy was one aspect, but devious gossip and
aggressive criticism had done much more to aggravate
Leo's overloaded schedule to the point of collapse.
I tried to console myself with the fact that even if
God asked for the ultimate, He had also promised the
eternal—not that it would be easy to let my husband
go. The possibility of shivering in an empty bed with
no hope of his returning home sent a fresh deluge of
tears streaming into the crumpled tissue.

At 7 A.M. I was jolted out of a fitful sleep by a
phone call. "This is Grace Hospital calling . . ."

I sat down heavily on the nearest chair. *So this is
what being a widow feels like . . .*

". . . Your husband would like you to bring his
toothbrush when you come."

"You mean . . . he's still OK?" I asked weakly.

"Yes, he's had a restful night. Hello? Hello? Are
you all right?"

"Yes . . . yes . . . I . . . I . . . just concluded the worst
when I heard you were calling from the hospital."

"Oh, I'm so sorry. I should have told you the
good news first."

My emotional equilibrium remained precarious
the entire time Leo was in the hospital, and not
just when the phone rang. Tears erupted at other

unexpected moments—in the laundry room when there was no Sunday shirt in the wash, at the kitchen cupboards when I caught sight of his favorite coffee mug, in the living room as I picked up stray copies of the sacred music he loved so well.

But there were little glimmers of hope to counter the anxiety—the reassuring words of a doctor, a clear X-ray report, and phone calls from my husband himself, his tone of voice conveying more than words could say. Above it all, there was a renewed appreciation for him as husband, lover, and friend.

That joy did not dissipate when he came home. If anything, it spread in ways neither one of us could have imagined. We rejoiced as timid hands from the church family reached out to help carry some of my husband's duties. These people grew in their faith and gained confidence in service as a result. Gossips were strangely silenced, no doubt realizing the seriousness of the situation. Criticism became constructive.

Looking back, I believe Leo's experience with burnout was God's way of impressing upon all of us the importance of *pacing* ourselves. Where Leo had to slow down, others had to pick up the slack. As someone wisely remarked, "God not only orders our steps. He orders our *stops*."

~Alma Barkman

For the Long Haul

All praise to him who now has turned
my fears to joys, my sighs to song, my
tears to smiles, my sad to glad.

—Anne Bradstreet

Well, there's some consistency here." I put down my pencil, looked at the columns of responses I'd carefully circled, and, again, consulted the answer key. This was the third standardized test I'd taken to identify my skill set and determine what career I should pursue. Since I was nearing forty, I was going through the process rather belatedly. That didn't bother me. It was the results that got my attention. Each test declared the same unfathomable thing: that I should become a teacher.

"We've got a lot to pray about," I told Joyce.

We had reached the point in our marriage where we both felt a need for a dramatic change. We were living in Alaska, where the winters were long, dark, and wearying. We worked at jobs that seemed to be of no real consequence. In my case, I felt especially dead-ended. I had been trying to succeed as a fiction writer, but after a series of promising publications in my younger years, the world, including my agent, no longer showed interest. How could I justify the unpaid hours spent by myself at home, scribbling words that, most likely, no one would read?

Spurred on by my test results and consultations with others, including our minister, we developed a plan that seemed straightforward, though the time horizon involved years. We would make a long-haul move with all our belongings and relocate to the Lower 48. There I would enroll in graduate school. After I had my degree, I could look for a teaching job at a university. We prayed about this decision, and as best as we could tell, we believed it was within God's will.

I wasn't naïve. I had never thought of God as a cosmic vending machine, automatically rewarding anything his followers venture to do in His name. And I knew, too, that God does not always answer even the best-intentioned prayers immediately. Taking that into account, I put my faith into practice and keep moving forward, trusting that divine assistance would arrive when needed. Through it all, I had to continue to pray. So we both prayed, and that's when the sky, figuratively speaking, truly began to darken.

We had relocated to the nation's fourth largest

city, where it was inevitable that two mild-mannered former Alaskans would experience culture shock. We were stunned by the traffic, the frantic pace, the pollution, and the rampant consumerism. The city was also in the midst of a record-breaking crime wave. Every day the local news brought reports of drive-by shootings, burglaries, carjackings, and violent assaults in broad daylight.

The level of crime was in part a function of the local economy. Business and industry were in a tailspin. Our plan had been for Joyce to support us by getting a job in advertising while I was in grad school, but agencies were laying off workers. Joyce had to find work, or as our savings dwindled, the reverse standard of living we were experiencing in our tiny apartment in an undesirable quarter of the city would only grow worse.

At the university, things weren't exactly going swimmingly. To gain experience in my future profession, I was teaching two sections of composition. Stacks of freshman essays loomed, waiting to be graded, and I had my own classes in which I had to succeed. The scholarly reading and the required papers led me to question whether I was really an academic at heart. Should I have ever contemplated this career change? What if all the prayers we'd prayed and the answers we thought we received had been a misinterpretation? Could I still make the best of things? Would I have to give up and admit defeat?

More blows came. We needed health insurance and heard of a supposedly good deal for people like ourselves with temporarily limited means. A well-dressed man arrived at our door with a brochure and forms. We handed him checks for several months before we found that no one answered the phone at the number he'd given us. We'd been scammed.

Then there was the day Joyce and I made it home just before the sky split open and gushed like a fountain for hours. From our window we watched debris floating in the parking lot, saw cars stalled axle-deep in water. The flood seemed biblical and symbolic: *You don't belong here.*

One night the phone rang, a rare event as we still had few friends. It was Joyce's mom calling. Her father had died suddenly of a heart attack.

It was our low point.

This was where, if I was going to be honest, I had to tell God that I was having problems with the concept of prayer. Why wasn't He listening? My tolerance was about to run out. I suppose, at that point, I wasn't unlike the disciples who dispersed during Jesus's trial and Crucifixion and the women who later mourned at his tomb. At such a dark hour, it feels as if there is little left. The best you can do is minimize the odor of failure by anointing the body with spices, then returning to the practicalities of life, going back to the way things were before everyone got their hopes up.

It's odd now to realize that during this challenging time, encouragement was lurking in an unexpected setting. I was enrolled in a literature seminar with the worst professor in the department. It wasn't enough that he had a reputation for laziness and not respecting students; he also relished voicing his strident atheism. Yet it was he, as a matter of familiarizing us with early American writers, who introduced me to a woman of prayer and great patience.

Anne Bradstreet was a Puritan and a rarity in her time. Married at fifteen, she sailed with her husband for the Colonies. What was notable was that she recorded her thoughts in poems that were actually published during an era when it was unusual for a woman to write anything other than letters or perhaps keep a diary. Even secular literary scholars would eventually be impressed by Bradstreet's verse and what the poems revealed about the sincerity of her faith, the way she humbly approached daily life, and her abundant love for her husband and children.

In one of her most famous poems, "On My Son's Return Out of England, July 17, 1661," Anne began her verse with "All praise for Him . . ." as a means of expressing her gratitude to God for bringing home her oldest son, who had been away on an extended trip to England. Anne had worried about him greatly and prayed constantly for his safekeeping during his four-year absence. On the day her son returned safely, Anne recognized that God had answered her prayers. He had sustained the young man, even in illness and during two perilous ocean crossings. For that, his mother gave thanks and celebrated in her poem "how graciously Thou hast answered my desires."

Four years is a long time. Reflecting upon Anne Bradstreet reminded me that I couldn't have prayer without joining it to *patience*. Not just run-of-the-mill patience, but patience that persists. If hope is the air that prayer breathes, patience is the solid ground it rests upon. It was important for me to dwell on that ground, not shake my head and walk away, my prayers reduced to a disappointed sigh. This woman from more than 300 years ago had taught me that I had to continue calling out to God.

The sky was already receiving some hints of light, though I didn't see them. For example, I took it as a matter of course that during our early days in the city, we found ourselves settling into a church. What was happening there was crucial, however. We had found others who loved God, loved each other, and loved us. Sunday mornings were a refuge from the violence of the world. I was grateful, too, for a mid-week potluck at church, with a drumstick plucked from a box of fried chicken, a dollop of someone's Jell-O dessert, and the conversation during the meal. Afterward, there was a Bible study where hard questions were asked and in-depth answers sought in Scripture. In this environment, I could confess to fellow believers my doubts and ongoing struggles.

In a city that on some days seemed harsh and unforgiving, God was already answering our prayers. Though the obstacles before us were not removed, He provided the resources to deal with them. Looking back, I can see now that even as my patience dwindled, God did not leave us alone and stranded. Through the miracle of His Spirit working in others, He was giving us Himself.

All that was years ago. Today we live in a hospitable, small city, where I'm a professor at a Christian university. Joyce and I have a young son who wasn't even a dim notion back in our difficult days of transition and change. As happily as this story of our lives has played out, I know it does not mean we won't face other dark times. That's why I tell myself to remember what God can do, will do, and has done, and to remind my family to always be thankful for it.

~Albert Haley

God's Upside-Down World

Lord,
Make me an instrument of your peace.
Where there is hatred, let me bring love.
Where there is injury, pardon.
Where there is doubt, faith.
Where there is despair, hope.
Where there is darkness, light.
Where there is sadness, joy.
Where there is discord, harmony.
Where there is error, truth.
Where there is wrong, the spirit of forgiveness.
O Divine Master,
Grant that I may not so much seek
To be consoled as to console.
To be understood as to understand.
To be loved as to love.
For it is in giving that we receive.
It is in pardoning that we are pardoned.
It is in dying that we are born to eternal life.

—Francis of Assisi

But that's not *fair!*" Willem's shriek rasped through me. "He got more *free* time than I did!"

I wanted to say, "He finished his math earlier than you did. It's time for science to start now. You had free time just yesterday, and he didn't get any." But I knew how futile that would be. An argument would start, I'd get mad, kids would start losing recess, and no one would get any science done. Instead, I smiled at Willem. "You're absolutely right," I told him calmly. "It isn't fair."

Stunned silence. Then, "So, waddaya gonna *do* about it?"

"Not a thing," I told him. "It's not fair. That's the way it is."

"But . . . but . . . that's not *fair!*" He sounded more confused than angry now.

"You've got it! Life isn't fair. And I'm so glad!" Everyone was staring at me, wondering what in the world I was talking about. "Did you ever do something wrong and not get caught?" I asked.

Grins and sideways glances met my questioning look. "Well, that wasn't fair, was it? But it was fun! I've sure done things I should have been punished for. But I didn't get what I deserved, and that's not fair. But I'm grateful for those times."

"What did you do?" Stanley asked.

"Hey, I won't tell mine, and you don't tell yours!"

I chuckled. "But right now, it's science time. Let's check our plants, okay?"

Lord, make me an instrument of Your peace.

"There really isn't much fair about life, is there, God?" I said in the car after school. "You act justly, though, and I'm glad." At home, I had a phone message from a coworker, asking if we could meet over lunch. She had misunderstood something I said, and she was furious with me.

"You're lying, Elsi," Carole said in the restaurant. "And you're causing trouble for all the people who trusted you."

"But that's not what happened!" I protested. "You're confused."

"You just don't see reality," Carole said.

"I don't need to take this," I said with as much calmness as I could muster. "If you want to meet again with the pastor or someone to mediate, I'm willing. But I won't stay here and let you verbally abuse me." I paid my bill and walked out, shaking. *But I didn't cry,* I told the Lord. *And I didn't start arguing and yelling, either. Thank You!*

"What happened with Carole?" a friend asked me later.

"Let's not talk about it," I said.

"That's taking the high road," my friend said. "I'm proud of you!"

"It's not me. It's a God-thing!"

Well, I'm sure not feeling love, I thought. *But . . . where there is offense, let me sow pardon. And that involves not spreading the story. Help me forgive and not make things worse. And, thank You!*

At church, the missionary in charge of the International Friendship Dinners approached me. "Hey, Elsi, can you help with the craft activity at the dinner next week?"

Oh, please don't make me! I muttered to the Lord. It's not that I would have trouble with the craft; as an old Scout leader, I had a multitude of good ideas. But I didn't want to have to deal with the language barrier.

Reluctantly I agreed. That Friday night, I took my plate and, pasting a smile firmly on my unhappy face, sat at a table. "Hi," I said to the Asian gentleman next to me. I looked at his name tag. It wasn't in English. "Um, what do you do?"

"Scholar . . . physics," he responded, and returned to his conversation in his own language.

"That's nice!" I said to the back of his head. *Help me, Lord!* I turned to the woman on my right. "And what do you do?"

"Journalism major at university," she said soberly.

"Wow! Journalism in a foreign language? That must be hard!"

"Yes," she said. "I not know what my professor mean many times. And my English bad, so my papers get low grade. My English not good at all."

"I think your English is pretty good, but maybe I could help you," I offered. "I'm a writer and a teacher."

Her face lit up. "That very nice! My name Yang Lei, but you call me Angela!"

We continued to chat through the rest of the meal. What fun!

Hey, God, it's Your upside-down world again, isn't it! I didn't want to be here. But I did it because You wanted me to, and You gave me a new friend and a new way to help someone! Thanks!

And I remembered, Where there is sadness, let me sow joy.

"This is the fourth Saturday in a row we haven't had any kids come!" I complained.

"What's the use of our being here?"

Larry, Vicki, and I ran the children's room for the Lamb's Lunch—an interchurch ministry to the homeless population of Boulder, Colorado. I was far too frightened of the homeless to interact with them, but I could provide crafts and a story for any children who came. And that freed their parents to help the homeless guests.

The few families who showed up wanted their children to learn to serve, however, so we sat in an empty room. Larry read aloud from his Bible, and we learned to play the Bible card games I'd brought. No kids. *What a waste of time!*

A woman stood in the doorway. She was dirty and shivering, with chapped skin and uncombed hair.

"What are you guys doing?"

"Playing a Bible card game," I explained. "Want to play?"

"Okay . . . it's too loud out there." She sat at the table. "Oh! You have papers to color! Can I color?"

"Uh, sure."

"What's this a picture of?" she asked, and we told her the Bible story.

"I never knew God did things like that! That's cool!" she said as she left, clutching her picture.

Guess we're here for Your reason, Lord, instead of ours. Where there is darkness, let me sow light.

"I can't believe you did that! I'm so disappointed in you!"

I had come to a decision that my friend disapproved of. She felt I had betrayed her, going against her hopes and plans. Allie's anger distanced her from me, so I felt betrayed also.

How dare she treat me that way? I fumed. *Well, two can play that game!*

But when I could get my head out of my emotional quagmire for a breath of air, I knew Allie was feeling as hurt as I was. What point was there in my adding to her hurt?

We had been in the habit of weekly phone calls, but I was afraid to call and be told how wrong I was. Instead, I called when I knew she'd be at work, leaving friendly messages: "Hi, Allie! Just wanted to say hi. Work's been pretty crazy lately, but I'm managing. Hope you are, too!" I didn't strike out at her verbally. I tried valiantly to pray for her regularly. I limited the number of people with whom I shared my grief over the broken relationship.

I think Allie was doing the same, attempting to contain her hurt and ask God for help. And, slowly, time and our loving Lord began to heal us both. We are friends again—a bit more cautious, speaking with care, but friends.

Grant that I may not so much seek to be understood as to understand.

"Will you lead the high school youth group?"

I stared at the pastor of the Chinese church in surprise.

"No way! I'm good with elementary-age kids, and Vicki loves preschoolers. We don't do teenagers!" God, however, had other ideas. With His backward reasoning, He apparently thought we were the ideal team to work with the students. "Lord, You're stretching me too far!" I complained.

One evening at youth group, a boy leaned across the table and demanded, "But why did Jesus have to die? It's not fair!"

What an opportunity to speak to his heart! I was so glad I was there, in that room, at that time, with that boy. *Father, give me the right words!* I prayed, and in a moment, I heard the familiar whisper in my heart.

"No," I said, "it doesn't seem fair at all. But, by coming to earth as a man and suffering terribly, he made it possible for us all to have eternal life. And all we have to do is love him. Pretty sweet deal, don't you think?" I asked with a smile. For it is in giving that we receive.

I don't really understand God's upside-down way of planning. When I take what I am given and return God's love in His way, it feels as though all the benefits are mine. When I give up what I want—the things I'm confident will be best for me—then God pours out His blessings. *Pretty weird,* I told the Lord, *but pretty awesome, too!* It is in dying that we are born to eternal life.

~Elsi Dodge

Note: Some names and circumstances have been changed to protect privacy.

My Search for Serenity

God, grant me the serenity to accept the things
I cannot change, courage to change the things
I can, and the wisdom to know the difference.

—Reinhold Niebuhr

In the fall of 2001, while most teachers were looking forward to a new school year, I received a phone call that jolted my self-esteem and changed the course of my career. I couldn't believe what I was hearing. "I'm sorry, but the position has been filled," said the voice on the other end.

The phone hung limp in my hand. I had just undergone several encouraging interviews and spent a day with the students. "B-but I was told I had the job," I stammered.

"Sorry, it was a contractual issue. We can't offer it to you." Click. She hung up.

That call sent me into a period of self-doubt and questioning. It was the end of September, with no prospects in sight. With three young children, a mortgage, and growing bills, I panicked. My husband's salary wasn't enough to provide for us. My self-assurance plummeted, and I wondered why God would allow something like this to happen. As the weeks wore on, I spent much time soul searching and praying for wisdom and guidance. The incident was devastating, especially since I had been through an equally upsetting situation only a few years earlier.

I had left a secure college position for a teaching job that turned out to be disastrous. Promised the moon, I was given the bottom of the barrel. This distressed me since I had thought this would be a good experience and a wise career move. Through these dark times, I spent many hours petitioning God for tranquility in the midst of turmoil. After eight months of intensive prayer, He answered my appeals.

The following year, I secured a leave replacement teaching position that seemed like heaven compared to the hell of the year before. I thanked God for the reprieve. I was told I had done a great job, and I hoped to get hired permanently. Even though several of the teachers thought I was a shoe-in, I didn't get it. I agonized over this as I had previously turned down an administrative position. Now, I had nothing. Had I made yet another mistake? I tortured myself with this question and others like it. I prayed, but I had little peace as I wrestled with these issues that battered my confidence. I implored God for wisdom but wondered why I was in this spot . . . again.

On top of all this, I recalled a disturbing incident from the year before. It took place at a school where a former friend worked, and she was on the hiring committee. She barely acknowledged me and remained silent as they questioned me. When she finally spoke, she interrogated me about the job I'd left. I wanted to forget the experience and move on, but she kept probing. I thought she understood what a difficult situation I had endured there, but she insisted on making an issue of it. I wondered why she had turned on me. What had I done?

This caused me to worry about how I interacted with people. Was I too pushy, too fast paced, or too me-centered? Endowed with a great deal of energy and creativity, I often did things differently, but perhaps I overwhelmed people. I begged God, "What should I change?"

His answer was not what I expected. One day, He brought my attention to a little plaque that sat on my porch windowsill. The simple, but powerful prayer written on it said, *God grant me the serenity to accept the things I cannot change, courage to change the things I can, and the wisdom to know the difference.* While I read it, I asked God to help me have that type of wisdom.

What things about myself did God want me to change? What things about me did He accept? Did I need to fit into other people's mold, or were there some real things that needed to change? Not only did I question my self-identity, but I also wrestled with the outcome of my actions. Had I been wise or foolish? From the world's point of view, I'd made a mistake when I decided to give up a good position teaching art to raise my children. But I wanted God's wisdom, not the world's approval.

There were many things I was uncertain about and wanted to change, but I felt frustrated. I'd left my job with the college and had come to terms with that decision. At the time I thought it best, so I had to move on. My coworkers agreed, and their support helped me to accept my decision. I couldn't change the fact that the ensuing job had been a difficult experience, nor could I change the temporary nature of the job after that. Even though I felt disappointed and hurt by those situations, I had worked out my feelings. Now, I faced another challenging situation. What should I do?

I ran to the Lord again and entreated Him for understanding. The Serenity Prayer became an everyday appeal. Since my identity was so crushed, I wasn't sure about anything. However, this opened my heart and mind to what the Lord desired to teach me. What did He want me to do? I'd been teaching for over twenty years in various capacities, and now I might need to change all that. If I wasn't a teacher, then who was I?

After confronting this issue and imploring God to show me the answer, I came to a very important conclusion. I understood one thing above all others: I am God's child. He wanted me to understand and accept that simple, but profound truth. As His heir, He had good things in store for me, if I was willing to learn from what happened in my life. He wanted me to realize my identity shouldn't be wrapped up in what I did or who I thought I was. I was a child of the King, and that came before everything else: wife, mother, teacher, artist, and writer. I found such peace in this knowledge.

He also wanted me to accept things about myself and about others that I couldn't change. He loved me in spite of my faults. I desired to learn to love others in the same way. Although there were some changes I needed to work on, such as not being pushy, God would help me with them. He'd give me the courage to change the things about myself I could not change on my own. Little by little, the truth of this powerful prayer became evident in my life.

I wasn't perfect, and He didn't expect me to be. I prayed for peace of mind and the serenity to accept the things I could not change. My path had been less direct than others', but that was my story. God doesn't make us cookie-cutter people. We experience things differently, though the outcome may be similar. My life and career path had taken a few more twists and turns than most, but God had something wonderful in store.

Several months after this soul-searching time began, I received a very different phone call—for a position teaching art in special education. It was a total surprise. I had stopped applying for teaching jobs in art, as I live in a college town that graduates many art majors. I'd been working in the special education field for over twenty years and had looked for jobs in only that area. However, the school district interested in me saw that I had art experience and called me for an interview.

I'll never forget the message on my answering machine. In a deep, rich voice that reminded me of James Earl Jones, a man introduced himself and said he was from the "Circle of Courage." I had no idea what that was, but God knew. He orchestrated all the circumstances. I went for the meeting and sensed it was the right fit for me. They had interviewed people from as far away as New York City, but they realized I was the one for the job.

It was very reassuring to realize God had wanted this for me. The job proved to be one of the most demanding of my teaching career, but He gave me the courage to face the challenges. I truly enjoyed teaching art again and working with students with special needs. God gave me an opportunity to help foster change in these young people's lives, and I saw many of them blossom. He also gave me the courage to change some things about myself. I learned how to "lighten up" and laugh more and have fun in this way.

Although there were also times of great difficulty, I possessed a new confidence, knowing I was His child. He would grant me the serenity to accept the things I could not change, courage to change the things I could, and wisdom to know the difference. I'm still learning how.

~*Anita Estes*

Reminders of Humanity

*Lord, be thou a light to my eyes, music to my
ears, sweetness to my taste, and a full con-
tentment to my heart. Be thou mine sunshine
in the day, my food at the table, my rest in
the night, my clothing in nakedness, and my
succor in all necessities. Lord, Jesu, I give you
my body, my soul, my substance, my fame,
my friends, my liberty, and my life. Dispose
of me and all that is mine, as it may seem best
to you and to the glory of thy blessed name.*

—John Cosin

Vicious winds swirled dust across barren Iraqi
desert. Sergeant Vicky Vernardo and I hunkered down on threadbare cots as our tent canvas
shook. We decided to sit tight rather than risk getting
lost in the blowing sand that persisted in permeating
our trucks and Humvees. That it was two weeks
from the conclusion of Operation Desert Storm gave
us reason to be cautious and not take chances.

A little before noon, the field telephone rang.

Sergeant Vernardo took the call. She listened for a moment and nodded. "Okay, Major. Doctor Hanson and I will get on it." She put down the phone and sneezed into a tattered handkerchief. "Sir, the Major called. He gave us a mission today."

I wiped a layer of grit from my scratched glasses. "Sir," she said, "Battalion needs us to locate a water-treatment plant in north Kuwait at a civilian housing area. When the Iraqis pulled out of Kuwait during the ground war, they tried to blow up all the wells. The government is asking our Division to locate the treatment plant and its water-storage tanks. The Kuwaitis are desperate for safe drinking water."

I stuck my head out the tent flaps and stole a look at the gun-metal gray sky. Low swirling clouds to the north caught my attention. I eased back down. "If this storm lets up, Sergeant, let's go."

By early afternoon, the storm began to dissipate, and we decided to head out to do the mission. Vernardo and I climbed into the Humvee. She took the driver's seat. We drove east through the Iraqi border and into Kuwait.

Soon we pulled onto the Kuwaiti highway and pressed onward toward Kuwait City. I craned my neck to look through a smudged windshield. "Sergeant Vernardo, watch out for bomb craters."

She clenched her teeth. "Sir, I'm not afraid of the bomb craters as I am about those unmarked mine-fields along the road."

I closed my eyes and brought to mind the battalion chaplain's comforting prayer from yesterday's worship service. "I give you my body, my soul, and my life, dear Lord . . . use me . . . to the glory of your blessed name." My reverie came to an abrupt end when the worn tires rebounded over a bomb hole.

A water-treatment plant stood off the west side of the road near a village of Kuwaiti homes. We headed toward the plant, stopped at the entrance, and climbed out. Shattered windows punctuated walls riddled with shrapnel and bullet pits. We marked the plant's grid coordinates on our map.

I couldn't help but notice a cluster of homes near the plant. They appeared to be housing for the plant workers and their families, who had fled their homes months earlier. "Sarge," I said, "let's check out those homes before we head back. Need to find the Emir to get his permission to send a water purification team here tomorrow."

"Okay, sir."

We walked over to the homes and approached the nearest brick structure. Trees and telephone poles lay splintered on uneven ground. We hobbled past a bullet-riddled Ford Taurus and a dented red bicycle. Deserted foxholes, apparently constructed by Iraqi troops, honeycombed parched dirt throughout the village. A few forlorn kittens and a flea-bitten brown dog wandered among bunkers, scavenging for food.

I moved toward the house. "Wait!" shouted Vernardo. "Iraqi soldiers are good at layin' land mines and hidin' booby traps. Stay behind me, Doctor Hanson, and follow my footsteps."

I followed behind Vernardo and stepped into her boot tracks as she eased one foot ahead of the other. We inched closer to the house. Broken glass lay below shattered windows. A splintered door lay on the ground at the front entrance. We stepped over the door through an open doorway. No one was home. Not even the village Emir.

A shattered porcelain sink had come to rest on the damaged kitchen floor beneath a gaping hole in the wall. The wind lashed torn curtains hanging on either side of broken windows. Pieces of porcelain toilet lay next to a hole in the bathroom floor. In the living room, an English-language New Testament of the Bible lay on a lopsided broken table. Family photographs were strewn across a ripped sofa. Broken toys, torn schoolbooks, and rumpled children's clothing had been scattered on the living room floor.

In front of the sofa lay a smashed toy airplane. A box of crayons rested on a bloodstained coloring book next to diminutive bunny slippers.

My mind went back to that Christmas Eve at home before I shipped out to the gulf. My son, Ben, flew his new model airplane over the sofa. Annie, my daughter, treasured her new crayons and coloring book. Tears flooded my eyes.

Vernardo and I looked at each other. "Sir," said Vernardo, "let's gather the photos so the wind won't blow 'em away."

We contemplated the pictures. A black-haired middle-aged man wearing a dark suit smiled in one. In another, a dark-haired woman smiled beside two kids, a boy and a girl. The boy appeared to be nine or older. The girl looked to be about six. The woman and kids wore attractive Western-style clothes. The children could easily have been the same ages as Ben and Annie. "Let's put these where the family can find them," I said.

We gathered the precious photos and laid them in a neat stack inside the front cover of the Bible. Sergeant Vernardo fixed her gaze out the broken window and looked at lengthening shadows cast by a setting sun. "Sir, we've done our job. Got a long drive back to the convoy. We should get going." She paused. "I wonder if, somehow, we can help the

Kuwaitis who left their homes here. They'll probably be moving back."

I thought for a moment. "Sergeant, I remember the chaplain's prayer from yesterday. Maybe if I write it down and lay it on top of the photos, they'll find it when they move back in. It might comfort them."

"How?" she asked

"People struggle for faith during discouragement and despair. The prayer might give them hope that life is still worth living. Even after war."

I sat down on a splintered chair, pulled a pen and paper from my map case, and began to write. Pent up emotions swelled as the chaplain's prayer flowed to promising paper. I ended the note with, "God bless you and be with you." I tenderly folded the note, opened the Bible, and nestled it over the photos. My dirty fingers closed the front cover so that the top half of the prayer stood in clear view.

We turned and stepped through the doorway to return to our Humvee. A gentle evening breeze fluttered through open windows and teased the paper. The dwindling rays of the sun came to rest on prayerful black print.

~Clement Hanson

An Angel in the Front Seat

Lord, Be thou a bright flame before me,
be thou a guiding star above me,
be thou a smooth path below me,
be thou a kindly shepherd behind me,
today, tonight and forever.

—*Saint Columba*

Our eighteen-year-old son was leaving home for the first time. In a few days, sturdy, dark-haired Bryan would pack his belongings into an old green Chevrolet and head for Oregon to look for work. Our family agreed it was a good move, yet I could not shake the fears that stalked me. My imagination ran wild as I saw Bryan's vehicle flipping end-over-end down a steep mountain ravine. Other times, I envisioned him lying unconscious and alone on the floor of a motel room.

Bryan is an epileptic.

I will never forget his first grand mal seizure. He was just thirteen, and I had awakened him early that cold spring day to do his homework. We sat by the dining room table doing math while my younger son, Nathan, warmed himself by the furnace vent. Abruptly, Bryan began to slowly twist his head to the right. His brown eyes fixed in a glazed look, and he fell to the floor, shaking violently, his face a dusky gray. I screamed for Nathan to run across the street for help while I held Bryan's head, trying to make the jerking stop. After the seizure, he slept for hours.

In the following weeks, Bryan underwent a barrage of confusing tests, brain scans, and doctors' appointments. When it was over, doctors told us the seizures were idiopathic, meaning "cause unknown."

"Your son should not play football, water-ski, or go swimming," the doctor advised, and he put Bryan on medication intended to control the episodes. We hoped the medicine would eliminate the seizures so Bryan could live the active teenage life he loved. But in the following months, the attacks continued to strike, and we knew medication was not the total answer.

"I can't sit around," Bryan protested. In spite of the doctor's advice, that fall, he joined the junior varsity football team. Early one morning, we received a phone call from the football coach. "Get over here right now," he demanded. "Something's going on with your son." Bryan had suffered a seizure during practice, but he kept playing football.

In the summer, he swam and went water-skiing, determined that he would not let epilepsy control him. In his characteristic reckless, nonchalant way, he shook off his fears by saying, "If I die, I die. I just want to do what everybody else is doing."

There were other difficult times. One day, he had a seizure in science class and, lying in the nurse's office, he told the teacher, "I can't go back in that class and face those kids."

The seizures often hit him in the morning. While helping our other five children prepare for school, I always kept one ear tuned to sounds from Bryan's room. Whenever I heard a dull thud, I'd rush to find Bryan half-dressed, wedged between the bed and dresser, shaking violently, his lips purple and pupils fixed.

I dreaded those times and often relied on Jenny, our twelve-year-old daughter, or my husband, LeRoy, to care for Bryan during the frightening episodes. Mornings were tense times at our house as we anticipated a seizure, yet hoped it wouldn't happen. The first time Kristen, our nine-year-old, witnessed an attack, she shrieked and jabbered nervously about what had happened.

When Bryan turned sixteen, the neurologist gave his consent for Bryan to obtain a driver's license, provided he took his medication. Yet, two years later,

the thought of him driving to Oregon left me terri-
fied. For five years, my husband and I had been tuned
for the sounds that sent us rushing to Bryan's side.
We had protected and watched over him through
every episode. Now if he had a seizure, he would be
alone.

I tried to reason with myself. What were the
chances he would have a seizure if he took his medication? Besides, he had come through past episodes
with only a sore tongue or a scraped shoulder. Unfortunately, my logic didn't vanquish the terror.

Two days before Bryan was to leave, my fears
closed in around me. Alone in the kitchen, I begged,
"Do something, God! I can't follow Bryan around
the rest of his life, but I can't bear to think what
might happen if he's by himself and has a seizure."

"Why don't you ask an angel to ride with him
to Oregon?" Rather than hearing the words, I felt
them.

An angel? I wondered. *Angels are only for people
in the Bible*, I thought, *for people like Daniel and Peter.*
Once, I had seen a picture of a small child trudging
alone on a dark path, an angel hovering overhead
with outstretched wings. At the time I thought, *In
real life, this doesn't happen.*

A Bible verse interrupted my thoughts. "The
angel of the Lord encamps around those who fear

him" (Psalm 34:7, NIV). I knew the words were not prefaced by "for first-century Christians only." A picture began to form in my mind—an image of a white-robed angel seated beside Bryan in his Chevrolet. I bowed my head and committed our son to God, and for the first time in months, I felt at peace.

Bryan left for Oregon. Three days later, he called. "Hi, Mom!" he said.

I felt myself go limp with relief. "Bryan, you're okay?"

"Doin' great!"

"How was the trip?" I asked.

"No problems," he said, and I knew he meant it.

I asked about his job, where he was staying, and if he had enough money until his first paycheck. Then I hung up the phone and leaned back in the chair. Our son was in God's care, and I knew he was in loving hands.

It has been thirty-five years since the day when I released my son into God's protection. Though Bryan continues to take medication, it has been far more than a pill that has preserved his life over the years. It has been God's mercy and grace in answer to the daily prayers of faithful family members and friends.

~Jewell Johnson

The Waters of Paradise

*Then Moses and the people of Israel sang this
song to the Lord:*

*"I will sing to the Lord, for he has tri-
umphed gloriously; he has hurled both horse
and rider into the sea.*

*The Lord is my strength and my song; he
has given me victory.*

*This is my God, and I will praise him—my
father's God, and I will exalt him!*

The Lord is a warrior; Yahweh is his name!"

Exodus 15:1–3

The blue ocean shimmered under clouds moving eastward. I gazed at the heavens, my body
bobbing and dancing with the Pacific, my nose kept
above the currents as I floated on my back. I had
arrived in Oahu from New Jersey five weeks before
and constantly had to remind myself; for the first
time, my Asian ethnicity was not in the minority
and, yet, I was still in the United States.

My friend had encouraged me to stay with her

while I looked for a job teaching English as a second language. Neither Evie nor I had known whether I'd find work—and a new life—in Hawaii, but we both thought it was worth a shot.

I watched the twenty-year-old surfers in the distance, their deep bronze bodies contrasting with the brighter reds and yellows of their swim trunks and buffed surfboards, doing their own bob and weave a little farther out. Each was waiting for the perfect pipeline wave. Patience was like faith to them. They had no doubt at all that the long-awaited wave would come—when it was time. I watched them stand, fall, and twist with the effort of maneuvering, and thought, *It must take courage to go out there and be tossed by such ferocious waves. No protection, no shield, only their physical strength and skill and agility.* I stood up and watched them closely, treading in the warm blue waters. *They must have special souls to be that brave,* I thought with a little envy.

I recalled the events of the previous weeks. I did land a job, teaching ESL at Hawaii Pacific University. As the semester commenced, though, I had come to forget Hawaii's lure in the first place: its natural beauty, the surf and sun. Instead, I headed each day not to the beaches and mountains laden with waterfalls, but to the cinder-block rooms of the college. My twenty-five ESL students, waiting to learn how to write essays and research papers, didn't know that their instructor was slowly beginning to self-destruct.

I had been drowning in class preparation. I'd sit on the bed in Evie's guest room every night, learning from scratch what I would teach in the morning. My confidence shrank with the struggle to memorize each new chapter, while the sinking feeling grew. I couldn't do it, I was failing, and I had no way out.

Finally, one night, I lay awake into the wee hours of the morning, tossing restlessly as I thought of my parents, my friends, my six-year-old nephew who said I needed to be in New Jersey. "So you can protect me," his small voice had said over the phone. He spoke in a whisper because his father—my brother—was in the next room, and he knew Rick's fierce temper would flare at the smallest provocation.

I was so far away from him, from everyone I knew, except for Evie. And she had just decided to apply for work on the "mainland," as Hawaiians called the continental United States. Eventually, even she would be gone.

That night, the tears came. I had tried hard not to cry all this time. But now, the façade of competency crumbled away, and all that was left were the tears streaming down my face.

"I'm so alone, God. I don't want to be here anymore. I can't teach. There's no way out, I'm stuck here for the rest of the semester, and I don't know what to do. Oh, God, I need your help."

My life was an evaporating ocean. Soon, I feared, only the bitter salts formed out of life's struggles would remain. The next morning, I stood before my first-period class after only three hours of sleep. My mind was as filled with sand as the Kaneohe Beach. This class particularly intimidated me: all males, all Asians, and no smiles on their faces. I later realized they remained solemn and silent out of respect. In Asia, no student would ever raise his hand to question a point, and he would certainly never smile. Doing so would show a feeling of equality to his teacher.

On that day, however, I felt my failure more strongly than ever. Unable to function any longer, I asked the students to check each other's homework and passed the rest of the class period in silence.

Depressed and exhausted, I hung my head as the bell rang for dismissal. I stood up slowly and began gathering the papers on my desk.

"Miss Wang?"

I looked up. Two students, Takashi and Reni, stood hesitantly before me.

"Teacher, what happened to your eyes?" Takashi pointed to the area under his own. "Do you sleep?"

I smiled, embarrassed. *I must look awful,* I thought. *Did I even brush my hair this morning?*

"We're just a little worried about you," Reni said. He had come from Malaysia and, like Takashi, wanted to learn English in this place known as paradise.

"Do you want to talk?" The kindness in Takashi's voice broke the walls of isolation that had built up within me. It was as though a wave of cooling ocean water flowed over the fortress, only to reveal that the walls were built of sand.

We talked for over an hour. They asked if I missed my family and confessed to feeling lonely themselves, being even farther from home than I was.

"I'm not a good teacher, and I feel terrible about wasting your time and money," I said after a while.

"Why do you say you're not good?" Takashi asked, surprised. "Other teachers make us work in groups every class. In your class, we learn a lot." He was earning his master's degree to teach ESL in Japan. "I think the most important tool a teacher has is a smile. If you can smile, it puts the lesson in our hearts."

"I'm only eighteen," Reni said. "Sometimes, people don't think I know much because I'm young. But I know prayer helps. Religion is my anchor wherever I go. Water can get very rough in the sea, but God keeps the anchor in place." He thought for a moment. "Do you pray?"

I nodded. "I do, but it seems like I only pray when I need something. I should really pray to thank God, but I don't seem to remember to talk to Him when things are fine. In a way, I feel like I use Him."

The two young men laughed. "That's okay," said Reni. "God wants us to ask for help. The Bible says: 'Ask, and it shall be given you; seek, and you shall find; knock, and it shall be opened unto you.' God doesn't get tired of helping us. It's just that we need to help ourselves, too. And what we want doesn't always come in the way we prayed for it. But, God always gives just what we need."

I had come to Hawaii thinking that I would help students learn English, but I also wanted them to discover that they had a friend in this faraway land. What I hadn't counted on was finding myself even more lonely and homesick and ready to give up than they were. And, just when I thought there was no one out there who cared, it was two students—in a class on writing research papers, of all things—who taught me that we are never alone.

The sun heated the waters enveloping me now, matching the temperature of the balmy air above. I thought back to that night of anguish. Instead of my inner oceans evaporating, as I'd feared, my problems had been carried farther and farther out on the warm waves of human and spiritual connection. Friends, I knew now, made the difference between a strange land and a home.

I gazed toward the horizon, seeing one surfer standing alone among the waves. With God, all we have to do is remember to smile. Then, we can all walk on water. I thought of how God protected us when waves crashed on every side. If we kept our hands in His, and raised them when we needed help, He would never look past us—not without giving us an answer first.

I thought about my family and longtime friends. I missed stopping by to see Mama and Baba on weekends, going shoe shopping with Amy and Gina, playing Monopoly with my nephew, Kenneth. Less than a month later, I decided that these were things I wasn't ready to give up just yet.

In November, I flew back to New Jersey. I had ended my teaching contract and had to find a job again, starting over while I stayed with my parents. I remembered my dream of being a magazine editor when I saw an ad for "Assistant Editor" in a newspaper. "Why not?" I thought, not expecting the phone message after my round of interviews: I was hired!

Nearly two years later, I still enjoy thinking of headlines and traveling across the United States to cover conferences in New York City, California, and Arizona. "God always gives just what we need," Reni had told me. Now, I believed him—and I was home.

~Christine P. Wang

When Faith Was Lost

Behold, Lord, an empty vessel that needs
to be filled. My Lord, fill it. I am weak
in the faith; strengthen me. I am cold in
love; warm me and make me passion-
ate, that my love might go out to my
neighbor. I do not have a strong and firm
faith. At times I doubt, and am unable to
trust you altogether. O Lord, help me.

—Martin Luther

There were only seven of us teenagers—ranging in age from thirteen to seventeen—who lived in the small, close-knit community where we shared the same school and church. We were typical teens full of life and dreams. We played silly pranks and shared serious moments from our hearts. We enjoyed hanging out together during good times and bad, fellowshipping often, and watching each other grow up.

The years passed, and as is often the case, life turned hectic and we became less connected. We focused our attention on the things in our own adult lives. Still, none of us ventured very far from home, and we all remained in touch, sharing the important news from our busy lives. Life seemed to be going the way I had imagined it should, until one spring day in 2000. I received word that one of our friends, Ava, had been diagnosed with a brain tumor. The news took the wind out of me. I knew about cancer, of course, but I had only viewed its destruction from afar. I had never experienced it up close and personal, but that was about to change.

When I heard the awful news, I did what I've done all of my life in times of trouble. I prayed. I prayed for Ava to be strong and well. I prayed for the doctors to be wise and thorough. My faith was strong and my expectations sure. I had heard it said many times that God, the Creator of all, is a tender Father, full of grace and love. I felt sure in my heart he would touch Ava's body and make her whole again. Believing was second nature to me. There was no room for doubt or fear.

One day, several of us got together and paid Ava a visit. When I first saw her, she had already been through several rounds of chemotherapy. I should have been prepared to see her, but I wasn't. The ravages of cancer and chemotherapy had taken their toll. Once a strikingly beautiful girl, with thick gorgeous hair, full of life and laughter, she sat in front of me, bald, weak, and frail in a wheelchair that seemed to swallow her whole. I felt a lump in my throat, but I managed to swallow hard and keep the tears from falling.

We spoke of old times and mustered a little laughter. Then she shocked all of us with news that she had just discovered she was pregnant. Although the doctors explained that carrying a child to full term might cost Ava her own life, she insisted on taking her chances. It meant she would stop the chemotherapy treatments and radiation, leaving the door open for the cancer to spread. Still, she turned her attention to the new life growing inside her.

Her news was bittersweet for all of us. What horrible timing; Ava had wanted a child for such a long time. She smiled and, in a weak voice, spoke of her excited anticipation of having a child. . . . I managed a smile and told her I believed all would work out for the best. We ended our visit with prayer, and although I don't remember the exact words of the prayer, I do recall that a sweet feeling of peace enveloped the room. My faith had never been stronger.

In the following months, I kept in touch with Ava and her family. We gave her a baby shower and enjoyed watching her excitedly open the gifts, just as every expectant mother does. Each time I visited her, I said a simple prayer for her to deliver a healthy child. Seven months later, she gave birth to a beauti-ful baby boy who looked just like his mother.

Immediately after delivery of her son, Ava's health began to spiral downward. We watched the life slowly ebb from her, and as she grew sicker, I prayed harder. Within five months of giving birth, I received the call that Ava had passed away. I couldn't believe it. Hadn't we prayed for her health? What was the pur-pose of our prayer? What good could come from her death? My heart ached, and I was filled with so many questions. Like water in a broken jar, my faith began seeping away, bit by bit.

After the funeral, I slowly grew angry with God. Just like the horrible disease Ava had struggled with for so long, an old root of bitterness began to grow inside of my heart. I questioned everything in my life that I'd known to be true.

Then, one day I met Jack. He was an elderly gentleman who had taken a job cleaning the offices where I worked. One afternoon, I had a chance to strike up a conversation with him. He pushed his broom while humming a familiar tune.

"Jack, what is that song?" I asked. "It sounds so familiar to me."

He stopped sweeping and looked up with a smile. "'Amazing Grace,' ma'am."

"Oh," I replied, and went back to my filing.

"Do you know that song, young lady?" he asked me with another smile.

My cold heart didn't want to hear anything about religion. "Yes," I said abruptly.

I could tell Jack knew I was trying to brush him off. Still, he was relentless and proceeded as if I asked for his opinion. "Well, the Lord is mighty good to us, ma'am. I know bad things happen to everybody, me included. But the Lord is surely good." I kept my eyes on my work, but that didn't deter him. "Did you know," he said, "I once had a wife and a little baby boy, but they're in heaven now?"

I wanted to be polite, but I didn't want to be drawn into this conversation. "I'm sorry to hear that, Jack."

"No, ma'am. Don't be sorry. You see, I didn't know the Lord back then. My wife was a faithful Christian lady, and she loved the Lord. I loved my liquor more."

I stopped my filing and looked at him. His eyes glistened. "It's true, ma'am," he said with a quick nod. "But my wife, Mary, prayed for me many times. Even when I found out we were going to have a baby, I wouldn't quit drinking. I was a mean drunk. Mary kept the faith, though. Then one day, it came time for her to have our baby. I insisted on driving her to the hospital. It was a stupid thing, but I did it anyway."

By this time, he seemed to be talking to himself. "I was too drunk to drive that day. I wrecked our car. I slammed head-on into another car. Everyone was killed except me. I didn't have a scratch."

I tried not to appear shocked as he told me about the accident. "The last thing my Mary said as they put her in the ambulance was, 'I forgive you, honey. God forgives you, too.' I couldn't forgive myself for a long time, and the law wasn't so forgiving, either. But I found out God is good. I'm here today because He is so good. You know, bad things happen when people do bad things, but bad things can happen to good folks just like my Mary. God isn't to blame, ma'am. Even He lost His son in a cruel and hurtful way." Apparently finished, Jack returned to his sweeping.

I was speechless, but I couldn't stop thinking about his words. "Bad things can happen to good folks. God lost a good son." For the first time in many months, I realized even God hurts, and I think it hurt him to see Ava suffer. The knowledge that she was no longer suffering gave me great comfort. Once again, I found myself praying to a caring God, who had always been there, waiting to hear my prayer.

~*Mary Catherine Rogers*

Rainstorm and Pencil Prayers

Keep on asking, and you will receive
what you ask for. Keep on seeking, and
you will find. Keep on knocking, and
the door will be opened to you. For
everyone who asks, receives. Every-
one who seeks, finds. And to everyone
who knocks, the door will be opened.

—Matthew 7:7–8

Rain pummeled the highway. I drew a few breaths to calm myself and flipped off the car radio so I could concentrate better. The ensuing void made my windshield wipers sound louder. Their throbbing THUMP, THUMP, THUMP echoed through the van like the heartbeat of a racehorse. Even with their fast swipes, I was having difficulty seeing out the front window. My knuckles ached from the stranglehold I had on the steering wheel, but I tightened my grip anyway. "At least it's not ice," I muttered, leaning forward and squinting.

I disliked driving, and I especially disliked driving

when the weather conditions turned sour. On ice, I never seemed to slow down soon enough. I tended to slide through stop signs with my horn on full blast, the only warning oncoming traffic might get before my van skidded past. Yet, despite icy or rainy conditions, I had never been in an accident. However, that wasn't due to any amount of skill on my part.

The rain increased in intensity. My son Michael sat in the passenger seat with his nose buried in a book, totally oblivious to the world. Somehow his quiet peacefulness made me more uptight. I imagined the disciples felt the same way when Jesus slept serenely on the deck while a storm thrashed their boat on the waves.

My daughter Meghan, however, sensed—and misunderstood—my tension. "Are we going to be late for dance class?" she asked.

"Maybe," I said. "But I'm not going faster."

"I saw lightning."

"Great. Now don't talk to me. Wait until the rain lets up."

Meghan had heard this before. I had little tolerance for small talk when driving somewhere new or when the road seemed unsafe. Talking distracted me. I had a tendency to plow over curbs, speed bumps, and potholes when I was distracted. Since scraping the belly of my van across concrete did little to inspire my children's confidence, they usually chose to remain silent.

Not this time. "I'm going to pray," Meghan said. "God can stop this rain."

At first I just scowled, distracted, of course, by her talk. But when the rain renewed its force, smashing outside like a truckload of marbles being unloaded, I said, "Go ahead."

As bold as a Girl Scout selling cookies, Meghan said, "Dear God. I know you can do something about this rain. So please make it stop because my mom is the worst driver in the whole world. Amen."

I couldn't believe what happened next. One minute, the rain devoured the road like a crazed tiger, and the next minute, it faded into a meek, mewling kitten. Just like that. I sat up straight and glanced in the rearview mirror. I spotted Meghan in the backseat with an "I-told-you-so" look on her face. "Wow," I said, and felt myself begin to relax. "Thanks. That's better."

While we continued on to dance class, I thought about what had just happened. It seemed that God had answered Meghan's prayer—and fast—but my mind also lingered on the possibility that the rain had let up on its own. Her timely prayer was purely coincidental.

I was not surprised my daughter had prayed.

After all, I taught my kids they could pray, not just at bedtime or meals or before school, but whenever they wanted. In fact, Meghan once told me she sometimes prays just to say, "Hello, hello, hello!" to God. However, I was surprised by the honest simplicity of her prayer, and by the swiftness and clarity of the answer. I knew God answered prayer. I had seen Him do so time and time again in my own life, but never so quickly.

It hadn't occurred to me to pray. After all, it was just a little downpour. Nothing dangerous like an earthquake or intimidating like a final exam or devastating like cancer or doubt-inducing like deciding whether or not to accept a promotion at work. Those were big-ticket prayer items—the obvious times for calling on God. I knocked repeatedly on heaven's door when the stakes were high.

Most of the time, I relied on my own ingenuity and resources to tackle problems, even in stressful situations that drained enormous amounts of my time and energy. Rain? Nothing I couldn't handle on my own. Now, as I look back, I'm so grateful God was a patient teacher.

Months later, I received a second nudge from God when my son and I talked. "How was school today?" I asked.

"Good. God answered my prayer."

I'm sure my eyes bulged. For Michael, school gets a good rating when they serve pizza for lunch or show a movie in science. I briefly wondered what had made him desperate enough to turn to God in prayer. Did a bully corner him in the hallway? Was there a tragic bus accident? "Tell me about it," I said.

"Well," he said, "when I got to class, I realized I forgot to bring my pencil. I didn't have enough time to go back to my locker to get one, and my teacher gives detentions if you don't bring all your stuff. So I prayed that God would give me a pencil, and then I found one on the floor."

I felt a sense of letdown. "That was it?"

He grinned. "Yeah. Isn't that great?"

"Are you sure it wasn't your own pencil that you just dropped?"

"No," he said. "It had an eraser."

Again, as with the rainstorm, the straightforwardness of Michael's prayer and the immediacy of God's answer struck me. It seemed like coincidence but, then again, so did Meghan's prayer during the rainstorm.

As Michael ate his after-school snack, I silently considered the two incidents. I doubt my mind will ever fully grasp how prayer works, but my daughter's rainstorm prayer and my son's pencil prayer proved how God not only cares for us, but how he listens to and answers us, even when we go to him with the seemingly trivial details of our lives.

I realized that, unlike my children, I often neglected talking to God in a simple and straight-forward way about the everyday things on my mind and heart. In effect, I preached the power of prayer but did not take full advantage of my ability to act on that power.

My children's faithful prayers stand as a challenge. Their actions remind us of something we may have forgotten as self-reliant adults—that we can pray whenever we want. Not just at church or bed-time or mealtime, and not just during a major crisis, although, most certainly, these times are important. We can pray whenever we want to. We can ask God for what we need, even if it's a pencil. We can seek God' help and presence, even if it's for comfort dur-ing a simple rainstorm. And we can knock on the doors of heaven anytime . . . just to say hello, hello, hello, God!

~Lori Z. Scott

A Time to Mourn
and a Time to Dance

I came naked from my mother's womb,
and I will be naked when I leave.
The Lord gave me what I had,
and the Lord has taken it away.
Praise the name of the Lord!

—Job 1:21

She was gone. Nothing I could do would bring my mother back. Lung cancer was the inescapable assailant. I was grateful that I had been there to nurse her through her final struggle. Later, as I grieved her loss, I recalled our last moments together.

"Mom," I whispered as her eyes tried to flutter open. "Don't worry about us anymore. Jesus loves you. He doesn't want you to suffer like this. Feel His arms around you? He is waiting; go with Him when you are ready. We'll be okay."

I spoke these words with tears my mother couldn't see, for although she had suffered long and was bedridden after a series of strokes, I fought against her spirit's departure. I had argued with the doctors, suggesting ways of getting her to take nutrition now that she could no longer swallow. I talked to my sixty-six-year-old mother each day while cleaning her room and making her as comfortable as possible. Each night, after bathing her and settling her for sleep, I would read Bible verses and, holding her hands, pray with her before bedtime. My husband of five years and our three-year-old son patiently helped as needed or granted me time to care for my mother while she stayed in our home.

But on this night, I knew she would not be with us long. Her breathing had slowed to become almost indiscernible. Somehow, my mother stayed calm, with near-normal vital signs, according to the visiting nurse. But it was obvious her body was giving out, and her spirit would soon depart. Thankfully, my mother was a Christian, so her eternal destiny was secure. But I dreaded letting her go, which is why I had to pray as I did that night, for my sake as well as hers. Pulling the sheet carefully over her body, which I had positioned with pillows for comfort, I left her after a final look of pity and love, leaving a night-light on before closing her door.

The next morning when I awoke, shortly before six, I felt it. My mother had died during the night.

Tears formed in my eyes as I lay in the bed, not daring to get up and see.

"Mike," I whispered.

"What?" he grunted sleepily.

"Would you please check Mom? I think she's gone."

Startled by my gentle request, he got up without a word, put on his robe, and left our room. I heard my mother's bedroom door open across the hall. A second later I heard my husband gasp. He returned to our bedroom with tears in his eyes.

"I think she's gone. You better come see."

With a heavy heart I prayed as I got out of bed, "Dear Lord, please be with her. Help me to bear this."

Following Mike into her room, I saw at a glance that she was no longer with us. I began to cry as my husband folded me in his arms. We stood there silently for a minute, musing on the awe-inspiring scene. "Thank you, Father," I whispered.

The days that followed were hard. I had been hired to teach at a community college about sixty miles from home, which required an hour and twenty-minute drive each way. Although I was grateful for something new to think about, a fresh start of sorts, the heaviness of my mother's loss sat on my heart.

Each Tuesday and Thursday I left the house at 7:30 A.M., returning at night by 9:30 P.M. Those were long days, but I tried to stay upbeat, grateful for the teaching position that could open future doors to a permanent job closer to home. Each of those mornings I left home with a purpose; each night I returned with tearstained cheeks and a melancholy spirit. I longed for peace that would put my mother's loss into perspective. Yet, somehow, I knew those dark days of mourning had to be fulfilled.

I began my new job a month after my mother's funeral. Between teaching days I kept busy caring for our toddler, Stephen. On Tuesdays and Thursdays, I left him with my sister and drove across state to teach English. On the long drive home as darkness set in, I would begin to cry, missing my mother's laugh and her sensible advice, feeling so alone out on that desolate highway. I thought my job would be enough to distract me. But sorrow found me alone in that car on those early autumn evenings, and I would give in, grieving for the parent I would never see again on earth. This unbearable sadness was followed by intense guilt for feeling sad.

"Please, Father," I prayed at last, "give me something positive to focus on, a new direction for my thoughts to help me past this pain."

Again and again I prayed, haunted by nightmares in which my dead mother sat up in her coffin, still alive. It was as if all the mental and physical anguish I had repressed during the two years I cared for her was now washing over me, like a dam of emotion that had finally burst. I didn't know if God would intervene—I knew mourning was an essential part of life to aid healing from a loss. But I kept praying, believing that God wanted me to.

By the end of the second week at my new job, I noticed my period was late. I was pretty regular, so missing four or five days was noteworthy.

"Take a pregnancy test," Mike suggested, excitement in his eyes. He had long wanted a second child, but after three miscarriages following Stephen's delivery, we had surrendered hope for another little blessing. Besides, I was thirty-eight, and having a baby now carried a greater risk of developmental problems. That wouldn't have mattered to us, as we would have welcomed any child. But pregnancy seemed unlikely in view of the fact that intimacy with Mike had been scarce and fleeting since my mother's death. I took the test, expecting a negative result. It showed positive. Shocked, I told Mike, who became elated. "Take another test," he urged.

I recalled my ob-gyn specialist saying that a home pregnancy test was about as reliable as tossing a coin. Nevertheless, I drove to the drugstore and bought another pregnancy test. At home, I took the test at once, even though waiting for morning urine is recommended to get the most accurate readings.

It doesn't matter, I thought. If it's negative I can always try again.

It was another positive. I couldn't believe it! Excitement now welled up in me, too. This was Sunday afternoon, so I couldn't call the doctor until the next day. Mike and I were thrilled. If only this baby could make it! We prayed right away, and I continued to pray until I went to the doctor and got a blood test that confirmed my pregnancy.

Our daughter was born in May the following year. I was thirty-nine years old. Despite an abnormal alpha-fetoprotein (AFP) test in the sixteenth week of pregnancy, I rejected the doctor's offer of amniocentesis, which could pose a risk of miscarriage. I treasured this special gift from God and would take no risks with her life. When she was delivered by C-section, I wept with joy, astonishing the doctor, who wondered if my epidural was not controlling the pain.

With my daughter's birth, God healed my mourning and taught my spirit to dance. For the first two years of her life, I anxiously checked on my baby each morning, praying that she would be alive and healthy. As she grew, I delighted in each new development, from her victory-shaped smile to her first, toddler's steps. Today she is a healthy teenager with an amazing resemblance to my mother.

Does God answer prayer? There's no doubt in my mind. During that turbulent period, He answered three special prayers: (1) to release my mother from earthly suffering, (2) to give me another focus to heal my grief, and (3) to grant us a safe and healthy baby.

God gives and He takes away. We can't expect certain answers to our requests or needs, but we can trust that God knows best. In all circumstances, we owe Him our unswerving love. In the end, everything will work out according to His plan.

~Debra Rose

The Right Place

Bless this house, O Lord, we pray
Make it safe by night and day.
Bless these walls so firm and stout,
Keeping want and trouble out.
Bless the roof and chimney tall,
Let thy peace lie over all.
Bless the doors that they may prove
Ever open to joy and love.
Bless the windows shining bright,
Letting in God's heavenly light.
Bless the hearth a-blazing there,
With smoke ascending like a prayer.
Bless the people here within,
Keep them pure and free from sin.
Bless us all, that one day, we
May be fit, O Lord, to dwell with Thee.

—An Irish Blessing

At last it was being delivered. I had been living out of packed cartons for five months while searching for another house. It hadn't been my idea to move from my mobile home in the mountains. In fact, I thought I'd be there for the rest of my days, but my children had finally convinced me that it would not be worth the expense to fix the old place, especially since it was located on a rented lot. Besides, the outside work was so demanding. I decided that my time could be spent in more meaningful ways.

So, the house search began. At first, we looked at fixer-uppers that, in my opinion, were worse than the home I had. We turned our attention to house after house that would require less work but found the prices beyond our financial resources. "Lord, lead us to the right place," I prayed.

I realized that I was sentimental about the old place, but I had good reason to be. I had often received missionaries, evangelists, and ministry leaders there when they came to minister at my church. In fact, I had lovingly named the place "Bethany House." Jesus had often been entertained at the home in Bethany where Mary, Martha, and Lazarus lived, and I, too, wanted to welcome the presence of the Lord and His people to my home. Now, I had made the decision to move, and it wasn't easy. It was a decision that had been bathed in prayer. Daily, I had asked the Lord to lead me to the right place.

After months of a fruitless search for what

I called a real house—that is, a house other than a mobile home, my family and I decided to consider "manufactured housing," which was really just another name for a doublewide mobile home. We were impressed by the beauty and upgraded standards of the homes, as well as their affordability. We selected a floor plan that was similar to a model we had fallen in love with at another lot, where the prices had been out of our range.

"Yes, we can build one to these specs," the salesman assured us. We found the perfect small, friendly park in a country setting, and the home was finally delivered. We felt that God had surely led us in our search. As I drove to the park, I visualized the bright sunroom, decorated with African curios that I had brought back from missionary trips to Kenya, and the cheerful small back porch that would look out over the spacious lot with a field beyond. I felt sure that many of the critters and creatures I had so enjoyed at the old place would be in this woodsy country setting.

At first glance, I knew something was wrong. Where are the glass walls to the sunroom? I wondered. And what is the porch doing in the front, rather than the back?

With disappointment verging on rage, I entered the house. "Oh no!" I moaned. "This fireplace is supposed to be in the sunroom, not here in the living room. By the way, where *is* the sunroom?"

Then we learned that the salesman's concept of a sunroom was to add two windows to a wall in a large family room. The home was in place. We had not been given opportunity to see it before delivery. What's more, there was no copy of the floor plan we had turned over to the firm, and we had not made one for ourselves. We felt there was no choice but to move into the home, such as it was. I tried to hide my disappointment. After all, it was new and, certainly, an improvement over the other house. So why did I feel like I had been betrayed? My family and I had prayed for the right house, hadn't we? This was not what we had selected.

At first, I avoided the room. It was not my African sunroom, and I wanted no part of it. I placed the newer pieces of furniture in the living room, seething inside because the fireplace dominated the wall that should have accommodated the piano. The older furniture was placed in the family room.

"Who needs a family room?" I muttered to my pooch, Maggie, as I placed her toy basket and bones beside her mat. She took one of her bones from the basket and contentedly stretched out on the mat. Well, at least she's happy here, I thought.

The unpacking process began. It had been my

custom to have my daily devotional period in what I called my "prayer chair"—a rather large, torn vinyl chair with a beat-up appearance. It didn't fit in my bedroom, so it went in the family room with the other older stuff. I would just have to break in another chair, I decided. That room was like a thorn in my flesh. How could I meet with the Lord there?

For days, I gathered my Bible and journal and went to the living room for my devotional time. I tried first one chair, then another, and then the sofa. Nothing felt right. Next, I placed a small chair in the bedroom, then in the office. What is wrong with me? I wondered.

"Lord," I prayed, "I asked You to bless my new house with Your presence just as You blessed the house I left. Why can't I find a place here that satisfies me?"

Silence.

One morning, just as I poured my coffee and picked up my Bible and journal, Maggie came running up to me with a toy. I threw the toy for her, and she retrieved it. Our game went on until we wound up in "that room." Maggie wagged her stub of a tail and flopped on her mat, but her dancing eyes seemed to coax, "C'mon in and stay with me." Laughing, I scratched her ears.

Oh well, I sighed, and sank back into the old vinyl chair. As I sipped my coffee, a familiar presence surrounded me. I looked around the room with its comfortable, even cozy appearance. Within me, I could sense the Lord saying, "I'm in this house, too. I'm with you always—even in this room."

I had prayed for the right place. Why couldn't I accept that this was it? After all, didn't He know what was best? As I sat in His presence, a deep satisfaction filled me. He was in charge of my life and was answering my prayers, even when I didn't recognize it. I had no doubt now that His blessing rested here.

The family room has become a different kind of sunroom now, because the Son is shining within.

~Penny Smith

Evening Prayer
of St. Augustine

Evening Prayer
Watch thou, dear Lord,
with those who wake, or
watch, or weep tonight,
and give thine angels charge
over those who sleep.
Tend thy sick ones, Lord Christ.
Rest thy weary ones.
Bless thy dying ones.
Soothe thy suffering ones.
Pity thine afflicted ones.
Shield thy joyous ones.
And all, for thy love's sake.

—*Saint Augustine*

She looked so tiny in that hospital bed. Only two months old, with wispy, light brown hair and eyes that hadn't decided to be blue or brown, she looked more like a fragile porcelain doll than a living, breathing baby. Since the tubes and wires made it difficult to hold her, my husband and I spent endless hours standing beside her, stroking her cheeks, her arms, and her feet. We touched her, sang to her, and prayed over her.

What joy this small creature had brought to our home! After three boys, the birth of a girl was cause for celebration. Her brothers adored her and couldn't wait to rush home from school to hold her. Michael, age four, was a bit disgruntled at being displaced as the baby of the family, but even he became upset if she started to cry and he thought I wasn't responding quickly enough. I reveled in pink bows and lacy socks and dreamed of playing tea party and Barbies. Of course, she didn't know it yet, but she had her daddy wrapped around her finger from the moment he held her.

Each of my boys had weighed more than eight pounds at birth. They were healthy, sturdy little guys with hearty appetites. Kimmy was six weeks premature and weighed only four pounds, three ounces. She was relatively healthy, however, and we were able to take her home at three weeks. She could take only two ounces of formula at a time, from baby bottles that resembled test tubes. She had to be fed every two hours, and it took one hour to feed her. She was attached to an apnea monitor that let us know—loudly and frequently—if her heart rate was too low or if her breathing had stopped. It was nonstop, round-the-clock care. Feeding, burping, changing, sterilizing, checking the monitor, feeding, burping, changing, sterilizing, checking the monitor—over and over.

We tried so hard, but her lungs just weren't developing fast enough, and we ended up in the emergency room at Kansas City's Children's Mercy Hospital. The doctors diagnosed Kimmy with bronchiolitis and admitted our precious girl.

For five days, my husband and I struggled to be with our daughter while meeting the needs of our three boys. We made repeated trips back and forth from the hospital, ensured the boys were fed and their homework was done, and kept track of the different treatments and many specialists. After only a few days, it was clear that Kimmy would be fine. Antibiotics had conquered the infection, and eventually her lungs would catch up.

But Children's Mercy was full of patients who would not be fine. Some would leave the hospital permanently disabled. Some would return again and again as they fought the diseases ravaging their little bodies. And others would leave the hospital only when their spirits departed from their bodies.

I began to focus more on the people around me and less on myself. I saw the lines of worry creasing an anxious mother's forehead. I heard the anguish in a father's voice as he broke sad news to someone on the phone. So much suffering. So many heartaches.

"Oh, God!" I prayed. "Comfort the hearts of those whose children will not come home. Strengthen the parents who face a lifetime of caring for a severely disabled child. Encourage those who have no hope."

For that is what Jesus came to do—to bring comfort and peace to a suffering world. He came first and foremost to save us from our sins, but He also came to share His joy with us. How many times in Scripture do we read about Jesus reaching out to "the least of these"? How many times did He bring joy where there was only emptiness and sorrow? He touched a dead girl, and a beloved daughter was restored to her family. He spoke, and Martha and Mary had their brother back. He embraced the children brought to Him and, in so doing, blessed both the babies and their mothers.

I might not be able to bring the dead to life, but I could surely lift those around me up in prayer. Even after we took our daughter home, I thought about the children who had remained at the hospital. My heart's desire was that every story in that huge facility would have a happy ending, just as ours did. Where that wasn't possible, however, I wanted God to make His presence known. In the midst of their sorrow, I wanted grieving parents and hurting children to know His love.

Today, our thirteen-year-old daughter fills our home with laughter and energy. Her makeup and hair supplies clutter the bathroom she shares with Michael. She's into fashion and dancing and all the things teenage girls love. I cannot imagine my life without her. And yet, I know that if our story had ended differently, God's grace would have sustained us. Somehow, He would have given us the strength to go on with our lives.

When Kimberly was nine months old, she had her final appointment with the neonatologist. We were told we could take her off the apnea monitor and stop the breathing treatments. Her lungs were fine. "Don't come back," the doctor said with a grin.

I may not have returned physically to the hospital since that last visit, but spiritually, I am there every time I pray for the people we left behind.

~Rhonda Wheeler Stock

Riding on the Wings
of Angels

Angel of God, My Guardian dear,
To whom God's love commits me here;
Ever this day, be at my side
To light and guard
To rule and guide.

—*Traditional Child's Prayer for Protection*

I rise and we talk. I thank Him for another day and then ask for His guidance and protection. Although there are probably millions of people around the world asking for the same thing, He knows my voice. He knows my needs, too, and He promises that things will be all right.

Our day begins with a two-part journey: the first, to the airport 30 miles from my home, and the second, more than 3,000 miles on a flight from Baltimore to San Francisco. I've traveled both routes several times, and each time, He has sent angels to protect my journey.

At the airport, a white-haired gentleman managing the ticket counter carefully verifies my seat assignment and directs me to the departure gate. There, I board a 757 aircraft, proceed to the coach section, and finally reach the row leading to my seat. Forty-five minutes into our journey, the flight attendant stops at my row with a cartload of beverages. "May I offer you something?" she asks.

I return her smile. "No thanks. Maybe later."

I'm sharing the row leading to my window seat with a woman and child. The woman appears to be thirty-something, and the child is about five. We exchange greetings, and I notice immediately that her husband and another child are sitting across the aisle.

"Do you travel much?" she asks, her red hair neatly tied back in a bun.

"Fairly frequently," I reply. "How about you?"

Her eyes widen in sync with her smile, and she answers quickly, "My first time."

"Oh, you'll enjoy the flight," I assure her. "I've traveled this route twice this year."

Another smile accompanies her nod of thanks for my assurance. I return to chapter three of my book, but a few pages later, I close the book and decide to study the clouds through my window. This turns out to be a short-lived activity, as my seatmate and her son attempt, once again, to engage me in conversation. "Do you have children?" she asks.

"Yes, two," I reply quickly. "A boy and a girl." Before I can speak further, there is a sudden bump, and the pilot's voice resonates with mild alarm through the loudspeaker.

"Please buckle your seat belts," he says. "Those standing, please return to your seats. We are approaching significant turbulence, and everyone must remain seated, with their seat belts securely fastened."

My seatmate, who identified herself as Maria, rechecks her son's belt and they clasp hands in a tight grip of love and security. Momentarily, I admire her protective nature, thinking how it mirrors my own.

"Have you ever experienced anything like this?" She searches my expression.

"Yes, many times, but not quite this rough," I confess. "Hang in there. It will be okay."

But the next few minutes prove to be anything but okay. Two more hard thumps, followed by dips in altitude, make the previous pin-size knot lodged in the back of my throat seem like the size of a fully mature grapefruit. I grip the armrests of my seat as the 757 shifts, first to the left and, then, forcefully to the right. Flight attendants move quickly from row to row, checking seatbelts and reassuring frightened passengers.

"Is this normal?" I hear someone ask.

"A little more dramatic than usual," replies an attendant who appears to be the most senior of her crew. "We are accustomed to some turbulence, but this . . ."—she is caught off guard by the sway and jolt of this medium-range aircraft—"is a little unusual." She disappears down the aisle, and the next voice we hear is that of the pilot demanding that all flight attendants take their seats.

Maria looks at me, and now, her little boy, Josh, clings white-knuckled to his mommy. "Are we going to crash?" he cries.

Maria struggles for an answer as the aircraft takes a significant dive and the moans of other passengers thicken the air. A hug and a kiss on his forehead quiet Josh, and Maria looks first to her husband across the aisle, and then to me. "Are we in trouble?" she mouths, shielding Josh from this conversation.

I reach across Josh and squeeze her hand. "I'm praying," I say, and she asks that I pray for her, too. I assure her that I'm praying for all of us, as I am certain others are doing the same thing.

We hit another air pocket, and the plane starts to descend. The cries from other passengers become more pronounced, and I look out the window, hoping that what now seems possible will not happen. So I pray more. I am seated over the wing, and my eyes catch what I perceive to be flickers of red. I quickly assume these are sparks coming from the engine. *Not the engine,* I say to myself. *Please, God, not the engine!*

The pilot, the pitch of his voice slightly higher, speaks again and asks that we remain calm. This time, instead of fear, I am reminded of my prayer prior to leaving home, in which I had asked for *His* protective angels. Now, as I fully take *Him* at His word, a sense of calmness inches its way into my heart, throughout my body, and deep into my soul.

Another view through my window tells me the sparks are no longer there, and this time, when the plane dips, it levels itself as if being steadied by an invisible force. The plane seems to float through the air. Many of the moans from frightened passengers have ceased and there is only silence.

Maria looks at me, and her face, previously full of fear, now looks hopeful. I meet her eyes, and then stretch my view out into the heavens. Instead of billowy clouds, there is a sea of what appear to be white, rufflelike feathers—spread out like wings. *Is it angels?* I ask myself. *Are these angels steadying the plane?*

Momentarily, I wonder if others see what I see, but no one comments. I turn away and feel the plane settle into a normal flight pattern. The jerks, drops, and rattles have disappeared, and only the roar of the engine hums through the cabin.

A few moments later, I peek through the window again, and the billowy clouds are back—broken by rays of sunshine. The flight attendants move up and down the aisles, reassuring us that the worst is over. The pilot, whose earlier comments reeked of anxiety, announces that we may unbuckle our seatbelts and move around the cabin. I ask the flight attendant what happened. Her puzzled look lets me know that she is clueless, but thankful that things are back to normal.

Maria and Josh lock hands, and once again, I hear their laughter. Her husband and daughter across the aisle resume their games of Old Maid and Go Fish.

Maria looks over at me. "That was scary."

"But God and His angels brought us through," I reply. For a moment, I'm tempted to ask Maria if she happened to see the strange phenomenon I witnessed earlier, but I don't say anything. All I know is that I'm eternally grateful I saw it and will cherish the moment forever.

"Yes, they did," she says. "God is so good, isn't He?"

Overwhelmed by the emotion of the moment, I can only smile and nod.

~Yvonne Curry Smallwood

A Heart Transplanted

Those who live in the shelter of the Most High
will find rest in the shadow of the Almighty.
This I declare about the Lord: He alone is my
refuge, my place of safety; he is my God, and
I trust him. For he will rescue you from every
trap and protect you from deadly disease. He
will cover you with his feathers. He will shel-
ter you with his wings. His faithful promises
are your armor and protection. Do not be
afraid of the terrors of the night, nor the arrow
that flies in the day. Do not dread the disease
that stalks in darkness, nor the disaster that
strikes at midday. Though a thousand fall
at your side, though ten thousand are dying
around you, these evils will not touch you.

—Psalm 91:1–7

Whenever we're scared, we pray—and my prayer was desperate. "Lord, I'm ter-rified now because I don't think I'll make it through this surgery. And even though I haven't been the person you wanted me to be God, I'm begging to survive." It was a bold prayer from someone who had rarely made God priority in his life.

Up to this point, I had done and said whatever I wanted, including my share of gambling and drinking. I seldom took other people's feelings into account. If they didn't like what I said, tough. "Nice" was not used in the same sentence with *my* name.

But now, my life was on the line as I faced open-heart surgery. I pressed on to pray and plead. "I'm sorry for the things I've done. Help me come through this operation and have a second chance with You and with my family."

The following morning they rolled me into the operating room. The doctors had explained to me the medical procedure they would use to correct my dysfunctional physical heart, but they knew nothing of the real heart change that was about to take place. As they worked tediously replacing several arteries, I began to sense a struggle. It was not a physical battle because I was completely anesthetized. It was a struggle for my life—but not my existence here on earth. Further, in the midst of the conflict, it was impressed upon me to read Psalm 91. The message was clear, yet my mind could not grasp its purpose.

Back in my hospital room, my thoughts, once again, turned to the sense of urgency about Psalm

91. A Bible lay on the hospital nightstand, but why should I read it? I'd never read the Psalms before in my life. Besides, God seemed to have answered my prayer and spared my life. The "message" now seemed irrelevant. I drifted off to sleep.

Several days later my condition turned grave. There were two blood clots in my lungs, and I was given twenty-four hours to live. I was whisked off for emergency surgery—a second life-threatening operation.

During the second surgery, I experienced the same urgency as during my initial bypass operation. The message to read Psalm 91 pressed heavily upon my mind. The operation stabilized me, and I was determined that when I returned to my room, I would find out what that Psalm was about.

My strength returned and I grabbed the nightstand Bible. I finally located the Psalms and turned to chapter 91. I read, "He who dwells in the shelter of the Most high will rest in the shadow of the Almighty." I read on about God's protection and covering, even through fear, terror, and the "arrows" that tormented me. It directly reflected the struggle I had experienced during my initial surgery. Was God reminding me of my plea for help and the fact that He had protected me and brought me through a tough time?

As I read on in Psalm 91, I humbly came face-to-face

with the fact that God had given me a second chance.
I had neglected to acknowledge His initial prompting to
read of His protection after the first surgery, so He used
the second surgery to direct me back to the Bible—the
written proof that He had heard my prayer and spared
my life.

Tears fell as I read on. "How come I didn't
get it the first time?" I asked myself, but I had no
answer. Perhaps God had used my prayer for help
as a reminder that I can't live for myself anymore.
I needed Him. Not only that, He wanted me to come
to Him.

The puzzle pieces were falling into place by the
time I reached verse 14: "Because he is bound to me
in love, therefore will I deliver him; I will protect
him, because he knows my Name."

This became a pivotal circumstance in my relationship with God. Before my surgeries, I thought of
praying only when I needed something. Although
I desperately needed God for my physical health at
this time, I realized God was waiting for me, His
child, to ask for His help in all areas of my life.

I realized God could help me be kinder, more
considerate of other people. God longed to help me
change other lifestyle habits, such as my drinking and
gambling. I also now had a desire to serve God and
others through church work and then, ultimately,

volunteering for an organ transplant organization. Through this, God taught me to acknowledge Him and His power to help me become the person He wanted me to be.

My prayer experience with Psalm 91 was the greatest heart surgery I could have asked for. In fact, it was my strength ten years later, as I underwent a total heart transplant. I had been waiting for two years for a new heart and one day the call came. A heart was available and I was next on the list.

My friend Steve showed up just before I went into surgery. He opened his Bible to read from Psalm 23. Though I knew there were grave risks associated with the operation, I believed God's promises of protection. Without hesitation I asked, "Would you please read Psalm 91? It talks about life!"

Now years later, it's my privilege to visit heart transplant patients at the hospital's request. I offer my experience as hope that God protects those who call on Him. Then I usually pick up that Bible on the nightstand and read the words that comforted me and taught me about God's protection. I leave the patient with a pocket-size card that contains a portion of Psalm 91. My encouragement is simple. Just as parents long to hear from their children, God desires to hear from us. He is there to protect and provide just as earthly parents do—yet even more so!

Through God answering in my time of need, I've found a further challenge. My heart's desire is that I not only call on God when I'm in trouble, but that I acknowledge Him every day of my life. For me, that's a true heart transplant!

~George Cop, *as told to* Karen Morerod

The Old Pierce Place

Grant that Thy love may so fill our lives
that we may count nothing too small to do for Thee,
nothing too much to give,
and nothing too hard to bear.

—*Ignatius Loyola*

I'm not sure why I wanted to return to a place that no longer existed. Maybe I wanted to look beyond the prism of life's distortions and remember the many facets that had charted my course in life. Perhaps I needed to relive a time of innocence, love of family, and the uncluttered sense of right and wrong. We had lived like gypsies back then, but to an impressionable little boy, this place was the most daunting, because it was rumored to be haunted by an elderly widow with a wooden leg.

I left the car and walked across a line of stones that someone had placed in the creek, and walked up the opposite bank. Remnants of the old swinging bridge loomed in the distance, its wooden planks gone, the abutments rotting, and the debris from a recent flood hanging from the rusting cables spanning the creek. Then I saw the semblance of a chimney, a concrete slab that was once the front porch, and the moss-covered stones of the root cellar. Over time, the house had been picked over and burned, leaving only a crumbling shell amidst a tangle of weeds and ivy. I did see what might have been the remains of an old wooden leg and smiled at the memory of things that went bump in the night.

This had been our home, at least for a little while, before the job ran out, and we had to move again. A never-ending cycle, it seemed: another rundown house, another new school with new friends, and another schoolyard bully to test my mettle and resolve. This was the place where a roller-skating redhead from Connecticut had captured my young heart for a brief summer; where Brownie, my black-and-tan mongrel, had died; and where I had my first brush of rebellious independence.

Now, trash littered every room and the foul smell of animal droppings, mixed with the musty odor of mold and mildew, drifted on the air. Dust bunnies, seemingly alive, raced before me with each step and fell in behind me like little trained fuzz balls as I made my way across the room. Lace curtains of spider webs covered the windows, and cobwebs hung from the ceilings like swinging stalactites, caught up in the breeze from a broken window. I remembered the stairway leading to the second floor, and the large stone fireplace in the living room. How grand they seemed at the time. I thought the rooms were enormous and the ceilings incredibly high. In retrospect, however, it was nothing more than a rambling old house, rumored to be haunted by the ghost of a peg-legged old woman stomping around in the attic.

I can still remember the condition of the old house as if it were yesterday: its water-stained ceilings, sagging wallpaper, peeling paint, and the irregular circles of water spots on the buckled hardwood floors. "We best get to it," Mama said that day so many years ago. She rolled up her sleeves and began the seemingly insurmountable task of turning another old house into a home.

My sister and I exchanged glances and followed her lead, because Mama was the queen bee where moving was concerned, and no one dared question her authority. After a week of scrubbing, scraping, painting, and wallpapering, Mama declared the house worthy of occupation. The queen bee had spoken.

Brownie and I sat atop the battered furniture and watched Uncle Woolyjaw maneuver his beat up old truck across the rocky bottom of Davis Creek, while Daddy stood on the opposite bank and directed him around the large boulders and sandbars. Once across the creek, he topped a rise and traveled a winding road through an abandoned apple orchard, past a dilapidated barn, and into what might have been considered a yard at one time.

Mama stood in the doorway and directed traffic as the furniture was unloaded and carried into the house. She cajoled, threatened, and complained during the unloading of her antique dining room set, a prized possession, and probably the only furniture in the lot worth a tinker's damn.

Later that night, I lay in bed among the unpacked boxes and waited for Mama to come and say goodnight. She walked into the room and sat on the edge of my bed. Then, she pulled the blanket around my chin and kissed me on the forehead. I wanted to complain, because if word got out about me being kissed and tucked in each night, I would be embarrassed to no end and would probably have to fight more than one schoolyard bully.

"How do you like the new house?" she asked.

"You fixed it up nice, and I like it a lot . . . except for the haunted part."

She mussed my hair and laughed. "Don't tell me you still believe in ghosts? Besides, as long as God is in your heart, nothing would dare harm you. Which reminds me, have you said your prayers?"

"Yes, Mama."

"Good. We must never forget to thank God for all our blessings. Speaking of blessings, I want you to jump on your bicycle after breakfast and invite Preacher Daggett to Sunday dinner. Tell him we're havin' chicken and dumplings. While he's about it, he might as well bless this house, because a house is never truly a home until it has been properly blessed."

"Yes, Mama."

"Goodnight, and mind your manners tomorrow," she whispered.

"I will. Goodnight, Mama."

She rose to leave the room, and then she turned and smiled. "You can tell Brownie he can come out from under the bed now. I'll allow him to stay with you tonight, but I insist he sleep on the porch in the future. I'll not have a stinky old dog in my home."

"I'm sorry, Mama, but I was afraid he would run away like he did the last time we moved."

"I'll make a deal with you," she said. "If you're a good boy and do your chores, I'll allow him to stay with you until Sunday, but he must be out of the house before the preacher comes to dinner."

"Did you hear that, Brownie? Mama says you can stay!" Brownie thumped his tail on the hardwood floor and whined, but he refused to come out of hiding until he heard her footsteps recede down the stairs.

Preachers must make a lot of money, I thought, as Brownie and I stood on the front stoop of Preacher Daggett's home. When I knocked, he opened the door with a flourish and peered down at me through tiny spectacles perched on the end of his nose. He looked confused for a moment, then his eyes lit up in recognition. "You're Clarence and Evelyn's boy, aren't you?"

"Yes . . . s-sir," I stammered.

"What can I do for you this morning?" he asked.

"I . . . um, Mama wondered if you could come to Sunday dinner . . . and we got another house that needs to be blessed. We're havin' chicken 'n' dumplins. Mama said that's your favorite."

"Another house to be blessed? Lord have mercy, I've blessed more houses for that woman than I can count. Where you living now?"

"The old Pierce place, sir."

"It's haunted, you know," he said, and laughed until he saw the bleak expression on my face. "Leastwise that's the rumor, but I don't put much stock in rumors," he hastened to add. Then he scratched his bald pate and removed his glasses. "Lord knows your mama is a saint, but your daddy, well, he never seems to make it to church. You tell your mama that I'll make a deal with her. If your daddy comes to church Sunday morning, then I'd be privileged to eat some of her fine cooking and bless her house to boot."

"Yes, sir, I'll tell her, but Daddy works day labor every Sunday on that new airport out near Coonskin Park. And since we don't have a car, he hitchhikes, and it's a far piece."

"Then I'll make a deal with your daddy. You tell him if he comes to church Sunday morning, I'll loan him my car so he can get his hours in. Besides, it's the Lord's day, and a body shouldn't work on the Sabbath."

"I'll be sure and tell him, sir."

Grown-ups sure make a lot of deals, I thought as I pedaled my bike toward home.

On Sunday afternoon, the wonderful aroma of Mama's cooking drifted from the kitchen as my sister and I placed the embroidered tablecloth and mismatched china and silverware on the table.

Once dinner was served, everyone sat down and bowed their heads in prayer. "Dear God, bless this house and this wonderful family. May they live in your light and sing your praises for as long as they may live. Bless this your bounty, O Lord, and as this food nourishes our bodies, so we pray you would nourish our souls. Amen."

As we began to eat, a faint *thump, thump, thump*

sounded on the hardwood floor. Mama looked at me and frowned. "Are you sure Brownie is outside?" she asked.

I hesitated for only a moment. "Uh, yeah, I think so," I said, and smiled.

~Stan Higley

From Mazatlán with Love

It was a warm Saturday morning in July, and I had just started clearing the breakfast dishes from the table when the phone rang. There was static on the line, and the voice on the other end had a heavy accent. "This is Dr. Morales, and I'm calling from Mazatlán, Mexico. Are you the mother of Robert Sorensen?"

I was immediately filled with apprehension. "Y-yes," I stammered. "This is Mrs. Sorensen, and Robert is my son." I had no idea that my son was in Mexico, and the rest of what the doctor was going to say would come as a total shock.

"I'm sorry to have to tell you this, but he was in the prison here, and another inmate stabbed him in the chest." He went on to tell me that the X-rays they took showed that the knife just missed his heart and lungs. "And," he continued, "it's a miracle that he is alive."

My head begin to spin, but I managed to whisper, "How is he right now?

And why was he in prison?"

Dr. Morales ignored my question about the reason for Rob's imprisonment, and curtly informed me that they could not treat him unless the family sent money. Then he asked me if I'd like to speak to my son.

"Mom, is that you?" The question emerged as a sob. "I'm in a lot of pain, and they won't give me anything for it unless they receive money from you or Dad."

Having been a single, working mom for years, I wasn't able to do much, but I knew his dad would help. So I assured Rob I'd call his father, and we'd do what we could right away. "Please don't worry about the money," I said.

He was still sobbing. "When that knife went into me, I thought I was going to die. Before I blacked out, my whole life flashed before me. And, Mom, I remembered what you had told me so many times before, about asking Jesus into my heart. So just before I blacked out, I prayed and asked Him to come into my life." The moment was bittersweet. He had nearly been killed, but then he had received eternal life. It was like the story of the prodigal son; only Rob hadn't come home yet.

He explained to me that he had been vacationing down in Mexico during summer break from college. And while camping on a beach in Mazatlán with a friend, the Mexican police had raided his van in the middle of the night. They found a small amount of marijuana and promptly put both boys in jail. On Rob's first day in prison, someone mistook him for an informant and stabbed him in the chest.

I had heard horror stories about Mexican prisons. I feared for his physical health, I feared for his mental health (and mine), and I feared for his very life. Beside myself with grief and worry, I prayed, "Lord, you know Rob's situation, and I know you love him even more than I do. I know that you are protecting him right now. But I'm sick at heart with worry. Please give me some assurance from your word that he will come out of this okay, and that he'll soon come safely home."

Although I don't usually play "Bible Roulette," I picked up my Bible and opened it at random. It opened to the book of Jeremiah, and my eyes fell upon Jeremiah 31:15–17 (TLB). I was amazed by what I read. "The Lord spoke to me again saying: 'In Ramah there is bitter weeping. Rachel is weeping for her children and she cannot be comforted, for they are gone. But the Lord says: Don't cry any longer, for I have heard your prayers and you will see them again; they will come back to you from the distant land. There is hope for your future, says the Lord, and your children will come again to their own land.'"

Since the Lord couldn't have been much more specific, my worries ceased, and I knew then that all my prayers for my son had been answered and would continue to be answered.

Through his dangerous and traumatic ordeal, he and I were both sustained and comforted by God's nearness and love. My family, friends, and I showered him with letters, Bibles, and other Christian literature. And he spent his remaining ten months in that prison reading God's word, witnessing, and sharing the Lord with his fellow prisoners. He also wrote and sent letters home that sounded like the Apostle Paul's when he was in prison. One letter read in part:

"*Even in this brought-down, unholy place, because of knowing the Lord I am finally a happy person. It took almost 26 stubborn years to attain peace of mind. The spirit of Jesus is so prevalent in my daily life. My newfound faith is helping fight my lifelong battle against moodiness and depression.*

The urge to get angry is unreal when I'm shut into a small courtyard with 150 other prisoners, with no privacy, no sanitation as we know it, and no virtue among men. Yet I say to you that I am able to be happy in spite of the circumstances because the Lord God causes me to be happy. As you said in an earlier letter, 'it would be unbearable without Him.' Nothing could be more true, and yet I am probably the only Christian in here. The Holy Spirit upholds me in spite of my unworthiness.

I think it was Paul who said, 'we shall glory in suffering.' This has been a key for my being able to handle it so far. Whenever I think I can't stand another second of this mess, I'm getting into a habit of thanking God and praising Jesus.

Please pray, Mom, that the Lord will grant me the grace to be able to influence others toward Him and that my life will be spared if it is His will, so that I might reunite with the family once again. There are people here who would still like to see me dead, as I am supposedly a threat to them, but so far the Lord has protected me. Since I returned from the hospital it feels as though He has given me a protective shield. So don't worry, just pray."

God shared His plans for my son's future with both Rob and me. "'For I know the plans I have for you,' says the Lord. 'They are plans for good and not for evil, to give you a future and a hope. In these days when you pray, I will listen. You will find me when you seek me, if you look for me in earnest. Yes,' says the Lord, 'I will be found by you, and I will end your slavery and restore your fortunes, and gather you out of the nations where I sent you and bring you back home again to your own land.'" Jeremiah 29:11–14 (TLB).

Rob learned to accept his situation in the prison and later said, "It made me a stronger person and a better human being for having had that experience."

God had promised Rob a future, and He didn't let him down. Rob decided to put the Spanish he had been forced to learn in prison to good use. Since then he's made many trips to South American countries and has embraced their cultures. He is now in a master's program at the University of Washington that will prepare him for a career in mission work related to Latin America.

I believe everything that happened to Rob that summer was all part of God's plan. He knew what it would take to draw my son to Him. And He knew what the future would hold. Even though it was a traumatic journey for Rob to find the Lord, I thank God that my son's eyes were opened. He went down to Mazatlan seeking fun and good times, but what he found was God's love, salvation, and a plan for his life.

~Gay Sorensen

A Light in the Darkness

God, make me brave for life:
oh, braver than this.
Let me straighten after pain, as a
tree straightens after the rain,
Shining and lovely again.
God, make me brave for life;
much braver than this.
As the blown grass lifts, let me rise
From sorrow with quiet eyes,
Knowing Thy way is wise.
God, make me brave, life brings
Such blinding things.
Help me to keep my sight;
Help me to see aright
That out of dark comes light.

—Make Me Brave for Life

N ow what do we do?" I shouted at my husband. I slumped down onto the sofa and began to cry. For the second time in six months, my husband, Derrick, had lost his job. "This job was our ticket out of here. What are we going to do?" I asked quietly.

"I know, I know," Derrick replied gently, putting his arm around me. "I don't know yet. But God does. He'll make a way."

I thought God *had* made a way with this job. Why would He close the very door He opened? It seemed like a very cruel joke after the emotional roller coaster we had just ridden.

Derrick went upstairs to change out of his suit and tie, leaving me alone with my thoughts.

Only six months before, Derrick was a successful marketing director for a startup company in Silicon Valley. The San Francisco Bay Area had been our home for nearly ten years, during which time he worked his way through various high-tech management positions. Two years into this startup, the company began losing money, and Derrick's division was the first to dissolve.

The dot-com industry was booming, however, and with his impressive resume, we knew he'd get another job quickly. But as he began searching for a new position, our hearts became restless. We knew God was trying to tell us something. The more we prayed about it, the more we believed our time in California was over. God wanted us to move, but where?

With a four-year-old son and a baby on the way,

this was no time to be out of work and looking to relocate. Fear and confusion latched on tightly and whispered their words of despair at every opportunity. Envisioning our future was like trying to see through the San Francisco fog. We had to rely on God for every single step.

We opened up a map and prayed. We needed direction—and quickly! I hated cold weather; Derrick hated the heat. My family lived in Ohio; Derrick's in Colorado. There was no way to logically decide where we should live. We had to trust God to give us wisdom and to be our light—our source of guidance and clarity. It took a couple of weeks, but after much prayer, we both felt Colorado was our destination.

We flew to Denver—where Derrick's family lived—to "scout out the land." We assumed if his family was there, we should be there, too. After a few days, excitement turned to frustration. "Maybe we need to pray again," I said to Derrick as we drove through a Denver suburb. "This can't be where He's leading us."

Derrick agreed. We couldn't put our finger on it. There was nothing wrong with Denver; it just didn't feel like it could be home to us. More than anything I wanted to be in God's will. What if we missed Him on this? Would it totally mess up His plan for our lives? Fear began to taunt me: *What are you going to do now? You've got no job and nowhere to go. You didn't really hear God.*

Needing a break from the stress, we took a road trip to check out a natural park with beautifully carved red rock formations in Colorado Springs, just south of Denver. As we drove past the city limits, my heart leapt with excitement. The foothills of the snow-capped Rockies were just to the west. Pike's Peak was so close we could almost touch it. A tangible sense of peace enveloped me, and I whispered to Derrick, "This is it." With the clouds of confusion clearing, I could shout back at the enemy voices of fear and discouragement, *The Lord is my light and my salvation! You will not defeat me!*

Shortly after our return to California, Derrick landed a job with a company based in Denver and with an office in San Francisco. He would train in the Bay Area, then relocate—on their dime—to Denver after the baby was born. We arranged to stay with Derrick's parents until we found a home in Colorado Springs, only a short commute away. God was working all things together for good, just as He promised in His Word.

Our baby—a girl, we learned—was due in less than a month, and our moving preparations were well under way. We didn't have a house to sell, since we never could afford one in the Bay Area's expensive housing market. We also had very little savings, but with Derrick's new income, we weren't concerned.

I had never been so happy about packing to move. Thoughts of our new baby and our new adventure turned the tedium of bubble-wrapping my dishes into a cheerful event. Joy, excitement, and peace overpowered the frustration, confusion, and the other adversaries that had recently inhabited my soul. Things were certainly looking up—until Derrick came home one day with bad news. "My boss got fired today, and they decided to reorganize the entire San Francisco branch. I'm out the door in two weeks, with no hope of transferring to Denver."

As Derrick changed upstairs and I sat in quiet solitude downstairs, the enemy voices attacked in full force: *Now you're really in trouble. You've got no money, no income, and a baby on the way. Your stress is going to hurt your baby. You can't afford to move. You're trapped!*

I couldn't allow stress to affect the baby. I had to force myself to stay focused on God and His Word. This produced a raging battle of the wills between my mind and my heart every day. Some days my heart won and peace ruled; other days my mind won and fear reigned.

The birth of Cayla supplied a sparkle of sunshine

to our gloomy forecast. But there wasn't much time to revel in the occasion. Our situation required desperate prayer for God's next step and deliverance from fear and doubt. I happened to hear a sermon about God providing for Elijah after he obeyed God and went to the brook. I realized our provision would also come once we obeyed God's leading. Our circumstances may have changed, but God's plan hadn't.

When Cayla was two months old, we moved to Denver with virtually no money. We lived in my in-laws' basement and continued to pray fervently for wisdom and direction. While Derrick job hunted throughout Colorado Springs, he worked as a personal fitness trainer in Denver, capitalizing on his passion for fitness. After three months of silence from the high-tech industry, discouragement and doubt came knocking again: *You should've never moved here. There's nothing here for you. You're out of God's will.*

Deep down, I didn't believe that. I had to remain confident. Not in myself or in Derrick, but in God. I knew that He alone would be our salvation. I had to walk in faith and not in fear. I persisted in placing my trust in God and, one day, He called me on it. I was reading the Bible and stumbled upon "Faith without works is dead."

"OK, Lord, You got me," I said. "What can I do to show You my faith?"

An idea popped into my head: enroll my son in a Colorado Springs preschool. School began in a month, so we needed to register him immediately. Everyone thought we were crazy for commuting ninety minutes one way to school, but I knew this was just the step of faith we needed.

It proved to be our breakthrough. After only three weeks of school, we "accidentally" met a wonderful Christian man who owned a property management company. He was willing to rent us one of his homes in Colorado Springs without proof of income or even a cash deposit. It was our "miracle" house that paved the way for a new chapter in our lives.

Six months after our exodus from California, we reached our promised land—and we did it with empty pockets. Just like the Israelites, God miraculously provided throughout the journey. Fear, confusion, and discouragement tried diligently to keep us out of God's will; but when we stayed focused on Him, He defeated their every attack. Derrick followed his heart and now runs his own fitness company, and the Lord blessed us with a beautiful home we can call our own. The enemies of faith still come knocking on our door from time to time, but with God as our salvation, we don't have to let them in.

~Renee Gray-Wilburn

Freedom from Fear

*The Lord is my light and my
salvation—whom shall I fear?
The Lord is the stronghold of my
life—of whom shall I be afraid?
When evil men advance against me to
devour my flesh, when my enemies and
my foes attack me, they will stumble and
fall. Though an army besieges me, my
heart will not fear; though war break out
against me, even then will I be confident.*

—Psalm 27:1–3

To this day, I'm convinced it was God's voice that made me jump up and turn around.

Hiking the lake trail near my home was a daily habit. I would walk two miles out, then stop to observe the sights and sounds and smells of the forest. On this particular evening, I was sitting on a boulder watching a pair of osprey swirling in a mating dance. An open journal sat on my lap as I noted every nuance of the dance and the sweet smell of spring flowers floating around me—hound's tooth, fawn lilies, shooting stars, and monkeywort—I was getting good at identifying each one. The mournful call of a loon echoed across the water.

A writer should know her smells, record her sounds, and note her sights. I looked up. No riffles marred the lake's smooth surface. A gentle breeze caressed my face. It would be another month before tourists would bombard the lake, stealing my solitude. When the sun settled on the ridge, covering the entire lake with a pink glow, I closed my journal and enjoyed the moment as a treasured gift. That's when I suddenly felt the urge to jump up.

A man stood directly behind me. "Oh, hi!" I said. He held a pair of binoculars in his left hand, with the strap tightly wrapped around his right wrist. Dropping his hands, he took a step back.

While questions sent my mind into heightened motion, I moved purposely away from him and toward the trail. *Why hadn't I heard him?* The forest was still. I should have heard the crunch of a footstep . . . unless . . . he intended for me not to hear him. But that was a silly idea. Surely he meant me no harm. *But the strap? So taut? As if he were getting ready to choke me.*

I hurried down the trail, wanting to run but afraid it would give the man ideas. This is a public trail, I told myself. There's no reason why the man shouldn't be here. Yet there had been no cars at the trailhead, and he had come from the wrong direction. It was too late in the evening to hike eight miles back the other way without a backpack, so he must have been familiar with the area . . . and with my routine.

Footsteps fell in behind me, keeping pace with mine. I picked up my pace. He picked up his. I looked out at the lake—not a single boat in sight. I was alone, a mile and a half from the trailhead, with a madman behind me. *Dear God, please help me.* Breaking into a full-out run, nausea threatened to stop me. The man's footsteps were still matching mine. *Keep moving. Don't let him touch you. If he has a gun, a moving target is harder to hit.*

Pumping my arms and legs as hard as I could, I followed the trail through the trees and around three different coves. The footsteps were still there. I could feel my heartbeat drumming in my head and arms. Perhaps a heart attack would stop me before the man would. My lungs burned and choking sobs broke from my throat. *No! You can't break down now. Keep moving!*

Reaching the first footbridge, I crossed it in short, quick steps. The bridge spans the narrow point of a cove where the trail makes a hairpin curve into it and back out again. When I didn't hear the man's footsteps on the wooden slats of the bridge, I dared to turn and look. *Dear God.* He was completely naked from the waist down, and his intentions were quite clear. Was that a gun in his hand? A knife?

I turned before I could make it out, determined to not let him touch me. The sobs came loudly now. Scenes from old movies and horrific newsreels ran through my mind. What would this man do to me before my life actually ended? I ran and ran and ran, calling upon God's strength the entire time and choking out the words of Psalm 27. *The Lord is my light and my salvation—whom shall I fear?*

It wasn't until I turned the last point, that I realized the man was no longer behind me. Still, I continued to run. He must have taken one of the many trails across the point. He could either be waiting for me at the last cutoff before I reached the trailhead, or he may have turned uphill in order to retrieve his vehicle. He could be waiting for me, even now, at my car. *The Lord is the stronghold of my life—of whom shall I be afraid?*

I slowed when I reached the cutoff, searching the woods for any sign of the man. He was nowhere in sight. Finally, when I was in full view of my Jeep Wrangler and saw no other cars, I pulled my keys out of my pocket and sped up the hill. It was then the anger hit me.

The man had stolen something precious. I would never again hike the lake trail in innocence—fear would always be an element screaming for attention—and all because of one man. My fingers were shaking so badly, it took me several minutes to open the door. I heard the rumble of a truck and knew it was the man, still coming to get me. . . . This time I was ready.

I started the engine and turned the car up the road, not toward home, but toward the sound of the truck. I caught the look of terror in the man's eyes before I read three digits of his license plate as we passed one another head-on. I was memorizing the other three on the back plate when his taillights came on. Stomping on the gas, I raced ahead. My home and myriad neighbors were the other direction. Only one house faced the dead-end road where I was now headed.

If the man forced me off the road, or blocked it, I had no way of protecting myself. Turning my Wrangler into the single dirt driveway, I raced through the open gate and into the cover of the forest. I barely shut off the engine before jumping out the door and running up the steps of my friend's deck. The house was completely dark. Then I heard the sound of groaning growls behind me.

Two enormous German shepherds were earning their keep by keeping a trespasser at bay. I was the trespasser. I inched back until my body hit the rail. The dogs stood between the stairs and me. The deck was too high to jump, which left me no way to escape. The hair on their backs stood straight up, and they continued to growl, but they made no move to attack. At least if the man came after me, the dogs would also go after him. But what if he had a gun? Would he simply shoot the dogs? Or what if the dogs decided to get me after all? Had I just traded enemies? "It's okay boys," I soothed. One of the dogs snapped at me. I decided to discard the calming technique and prayed for God to quiet the animals.

I looked past the dogs and watched for headlights. I hoped the man would think the owners were home and calling 911. I waited, wishing the dogs would leave and praying the man would not come. Frigid cold tainted the air. Night turned as black as an abandoned well. Finally, the dogs moved to the other side of the stairs. I inched my way forward and down to my car, thinking of nothing but reaching home. The turnoff to my little rural neighborhood was less than a mile away. I soon turned onto our street and stopped.

I couldn't go home. What if he was there? What if he knew where I lived? My husband, Cat, should be on his way home from work by now, but it would be another hour before he would reach me. *A lot of things could happen in an hour.* I shuddered and turned into another neighbor's driveway. When Gayle and Jim opened the door, I fell apart.

When I look back, I realize God gave me the strength and courage to make it through the entire ordeal. I was terribly out of shape at the time, yet God kept me running. When everything in me wanted to give up and sit down and bawl, God's gentle but firm voice was ever present, urging me on. He protected me in that dark hour and made a stronghold around me in the coming weeks before the evil man was arrested. After his arrest, God gave me the strength to testify against my attacker and ask that the court get help for him.

Today, I continue to hike the lake trail, and whenever I feel fear, I quote the words of Psalm 27. Each and every time, my heart settles in perfect peace. That kind of freedom from fear can only come from our amazing God.

~Sandy Cathcart

Morning Prayer of a Homemaker

*Even though I clutch my blanket and growl
when the alarm rings, thank You, Lord, that
I can hear. There are many who are deaf.
Even though I keep my eyes closed against
the morning light as long as possible, thank
You, Lord, that I can see. Many are blind.
Even though I huddle in my bed and put
off rising, thank You, Lord, that I have the
strength to rise. There are many who are
bedridden. Even though my children are so
loud, thank You, Lord, for my family. There
are many who are lonely. Even though our
breakfast table never looks like the pictures
in magazines and the menu is at times not
balanced, there are many who are hungry.
Even though the routine of my job is often
monotonous, thank You, Lord, for the
opportunity to work. There are many who
have no job. Thank You, Lord, for life.*

—Morning Prayer of a Homemaker

light rain misted the windshield as I drove to the mall for the umpteenth time. As I skidded to a stop at a red light, I mentally calculated the cost of new brake pads. I was completely distracted, and that was before chaos engulfed the backseat. The voices of my three daughters rose in a familiar chorus of arguments and complaints. My throat tightened, and I felt my heart beating faster. My head was pounding. I was so tired of their constant squabbling. Before I could stop myself, I joined the horrible racket with my own yelling. "Stop it—just stop it! All three of you!" Startled into silence by my uncharacteristic outburst, the girls were fairly subdued for the rest of the afternoon.

Later that evening, I told my husband about my outburst. "I just don't think I can take their arguing anymore," I told him, a little whiny myself. "It's nonstop. They argue constantly, about every little thing. I just wish they could get along. I'm ready for a break."

He smiled at me, nodding in sympathy. Then, he shook his head. "Remember when you didn't have them?" he asked softly. "Remember when the doctors said we'd never have any children?" I remained silent, remembering, as he continued. "What if they'd never been born at all? Would it be better to have peace and quiet than to have the girls?"

My eyes filled with tears. I didn't answer him right away, but I was taking in every word. I knew that he was absolutely right. Having my babies had been a huge miracle, and I thought back thirteen years to that blessed turning point in our lives.

I'd been to three specialists in one month, and they all had the same news—no children. I was infertile. I had suffered from severe endometriosis, but even after surgery, I was still unable to conceive. The doctors weren't sure why, but they said the scar tissue from the endometriosis and the surgery to correct it had irreparably damaged my reproductive organs. "You might as well adopt," one doctor advised curtly, slamming my medical chart shut, "because you will never, ever be able to have babies on your own."

And then my sister gave me a small book, *Hung by the Tongue*, by Francis Marion. It was about prayer and the enormous power of positive confession. I read it in one afternoon and was stunned. Could it be possible that my negative words had decreased my ability to conceive even more? And, more importantly, was it true that if I could speak out the positive and pray in the affirmative, I might have a chance at changing my inability to become pregnant?

That afternoon, I walked down to the lake behind my in-laws' home. My husband was up at the driveway, washing cars for our families. I could hear him whistling as I sat down at the cement picnic table by the water. Closing my eyes, I took a deep breath and began to pray. "Dearest Father," I said, "if it's true that our words can affect our lives, then please forgive me for the negative way I've spoken about my desire for a baby. Father, You can do whatever You want in my life. I surrender it to You now. If You want me to be a mother, I will be one. And if You don't, I pray You will give me peace to accept it. But either way, help me from this moment on, only to speak positive, uplifting words about my life and the lives of my loved ones. I love You, Lord. In Jesus's name I pray, Amen."

Two weeks later, I realized my period was late. That never happened to me. I prayed quickly for God to be with me as I ran to the nearest drugstore. It was almost 10 P.M. My husband was out of state at a work conference. I'd taken lots of pregnancy tests before, and they had always been negative. But this time—this time I had a little flicker of hope before I even took the test. When I picked it up after three minutes, my heart was beating so fast I could hardly breathe. And there they were. Two glorious blue lines. Not one, but two. I was pregnant. Finally!

The sound of voices escalating in the next room brought me back to the present. I recognized the voice of my youngest daughter, Caroline, first. "Give it back," she whined. Before I could get to the next room, I heard my oldest child, Zoe, and my middle girl, Chloe, chiming in. "It's not yours," Zoe announced in a bossy voice. "Mama gave it to me first!" countered Chloe.

The familiar reaction rose up within me: pounding heart, choked throat, tension headache. But this time, something else stirred in me as well. It took me a minute to identify the strange new emotion coursing through my heart. And then I knew for certain; it was gratitude. I was actually thankful to hear my daughters arguing once again.

I smiled. I might, indeed, have a chaotic, whirlwind life with my lively, rambunctious girls. True, they did fight too much, and it was exhausting trying to referee every battle. But the thought of the alternative, of a quiet, calm life without them in it, was intolerable. I realized that, while I'm often stressed to the max with the noise and confusion, there is one thing I rarely am, and that's lonely. I'm surrounded by life—vibrant, colorful, noisy, and confusing, but oh, so rich and full and beautiful.

I made another mental note. This one was to remind me to thank their father for his wisdom and insight, and to thank my heavenly Father for teaching me how to be grateful for my life, in all its ordinary, wild and woolly ways.

That night, as my three little girls lay sleeping, I stood in their doorways and gazed down at them. They were so beautiful lying there, and I realized that what I had learned didn't just apply to them. It applied to every single area of my life.

Though there are many times I do not feel up to meeting each new day, though I dread the inevitable conflicts and crises, I know—deeply, and with a growing new assurance—that I need to be thankful, every morning, every night, no matter what. Then, whatever comes my way, I'll accept it with poise, grace, and confidence. I know that everything is from my Lord and is for my ultimate good.

~Donna Surgenor Reames

Green Lights from God

*Almighty God, in whom we live and move
and have our being, you have made us for
yourself, and our hearts are restless until
they find their rest in you. Grant us purity
of heart and strength of purpose so that no
other passion may hinder us from knowing your will, no weakness from doing it.*

—*Augustine of Hippo*

My husband, Lloyd, and I dreamed of sending our children to a Christian school. We
had only one income, but we remained focused and
sacrificed until we could afford tuition. Now, after
five years of sending our children to the school at our
church, our dream was dissolving.

Our church had started the school the same
year our oldest son entered kindergarten. When we
enrolled Josiah, we didn't know what to expect, but
we hoped the academics would be on par with public schools, with the bonus of Christianity woven
throughout the curriculum. We also hoped for a

positive social environment where our children would grow in the faith and make Christian friends.

The school had kind teachers and a focus on the faith, but it also had a contingent of parents who expressed the view that "I'm not paying $4,000 a year just to have my child learn about Jesus. They can learn that in Sunday school. What I want for my child is an education that's better than that of public schools."

Slowly, the school became more and more focused on academic superiority. Parents talked as if winning scholarships and attending Ivy League universities were their main goals in having their children attend the school. And these children were only in the elementary grades.

Lloyd and I struggled with this attitude. If our children wanted to go to an Ivy League university someday, we'd do our best to make it a reality, but that had never been our goal in sending them to a Christian school. We weren't sure it should even be our goal to see them become professionals. Jesus had been a carpenter. Most of his closest disciples were fishermen.

Our school soon hired an administrator who worked to further establish the facility as an elite academy. One of his first steps was to raise tuition several hundred dollars. Class sizes had been dwindling, and now, even fewer families found they could afford the school. Josiah's class, which had started with twelve students, would be reduced to only three. Lloyd and I found ourselves at odds with the school's increasing exclusivity—hadn't Jesus welcomed the poor and children?

In addition to these troubles, our commute to the church took a half hour, so, on school days, I was driving an hour every morning and every afternoon. If Lloyd and I wanted to continue sending our children to this school, I might need to find a job, but what kind of job could I find with hours like that?

Even before the arrival of the new administrator, Lloyd and I had decided to move closer to the school, but now we wondered if we should switch to another school. We prayed for guidance. I began visiting other Christian schools in Kansas City. I found one we liked, but the commute was even longer than the one we had now. As a child, I had experienced a vision in which I was an author living in a redbrick house. None of these houses were brick or looked anything like the one in my vision.

Lloyd had always wanted to live in Nebraska, where he grew up. We felt tied to Kansas City because the company he worked for had hired him to establish a presence in Kansas City. But after praying about it, I suggested he ask his boss if we could move to Nebraska.

"That'll never fly," Lloyd said.

Secretly, I was a bit relieved. I felt God might be nudging us toward Nebraska, but our best friends were at our church in Kansas City. We had thirteen years invested in those friendships: starting out together as newlyweds, throwing housewarming parties for one another, delivering meals with the birth of each child, being there in medical emergencies and late-night crises. I didn't want to leave these special friends.

A few days later, though, Lloyd had news: "My boss said we could move to Nebraska."

"But how can that be?" I asked.

"I reminded him that they hired me for Kansas City, but he doesn't remember that. He checked with upper management, and they okayed a move to Nebraska."

I hedged. "Now that it's a reality, I'm not sure I want to move."

"I know," Lloyd said. "We could end up in a worse situation."

"But when you pray to God for guidance and you get it, what do you do . . . ignore it?"

"You take it," he said.

We drove to Lincoln, Nebraska, a couple of

weekends after that, in January. We toured the town and discovered four Christian schools. We were wowed by the schools and felt any one of them could be the home away from home we wanted for our children.

I was also awed by all the brick I saw around town. We didn't want to move anywhere until school was out, but we decided to check the housing market anyway. We located a real estate agent, and he told us that brick houses in Lincoln were common and affordable because there were two brickyards just outside the town, and they were in competition with each other. He gave us a list of thirty houses that met our criteria.

Lloyd and I each looked at our own copy of the list and separately ranked our top picks. Our lists were close to matching—which was almost miraculous because Lloyd and I are seldom on the same wavelength. What's more, our number one picks matched, and so did our number two picks. And when we toured the number one pick, we both agreed we wanted it. So we bought our redbrick house.

The decision to move to another state to find the best Christian school for our children was risky. We suffered financial losses in selling our house and moving, but we were convinced that it was God's will for us to move. This belief has been confirmed for us repeatedly since our move.

One of the first confirmations came in a sermon preached at our new church. The pastor centered the sermon on Acts 17:26–27: "From one man God made every nation of men, that they should inhabit the whole earth; and he determined the times set for them and the exact places where they should live. God did this so that men would seek him and perhaps reach out for him and find him, though he is not far from each one of us."

We soon learned that our new pastor was the brother of the pastor who married us—even though their home state was Florida. Friends we had from years ago, but with whom we had lost touch, turned out to be living in Lincoln. And we made new friends when our church ushered us into a small-group Bible study.

The most recent confirmation came when I signed contracts for four children's books. I have become the "author in a redbrick house" from my childhood vision.

~Ronica Stromberg

The Faith We Shared

I feel a strong immortal hope
Which bears my mournful spirit up
Beneath its mountain load;
Redeemed from death, and grief, and pain,
I soon shall find my friend again
Within the arms of God.
Pass a few fleeting moments more
And death the blessing shall restore
Which death has snatched away;
For me You will the summons send,
And give me back my parted friend
In that eternal day.

—*Charles Wesley*

The pungent scent of garlic and onions, sizzling in olive oil, woke me from a deep sleep. I smiled and thought, Nana must be here. Then reality covered me like a thick blanket. Nana couldn't be here. She had died a week ago, from complications of severe scoliosis and emphysema. I'd returned from her funeral several hours ago. My roommate,

Liz, remembering that my grandmother, whom I affectionately called "Nana," had loved to cook Italian food, was probably making spaghetti sauce from scratch to ease my pain.

She couldn't know how much the familiar smell hurt me. It brought home the realization that Nana would never again stand for hours over the stove, loving her special spaghetti sauce into creation. She would never again dip a bit of Italian bread into the scarlet sauce, blow on it, and offer it to me. So the smell of the sauce cooking in our kitchen brought pain and grief instead of the usual delight and pleasure.

Still, I tried to put on a cheerful face when Liz tapped on my bedroom door to tell me she'd made spaghetti. "How thoughtful of you!" I said as I sampled her delicious sauce and nibbled strands of spaghetti. Inwardly, I cringed. This wasn't Nana's sauce! Even if it had tasted exactly like hers, the fact that Nana could no longer share it with me made my stomach clench in protest. Finally I pushed away my half-finished plate.

"Thanks, Liz," I said. "Your spaghetti's great. I guess I'm just not hungry."

When I was a young child, Nana's house was a refuge for me. My parents, both children of alcoholics, threw fear and anger around the house like Ping-

Pong balls. Though they didn't drink, they used my siblings and me as weapons in their emotional wars.

Nana was a tiny woman filled with quiet strength and determination. When my grandfather died of lung cancer, she worked in a bank to keep a roof over my aunt and uncle's heads. She had a sense of dignity that precluded her becoming directly involved in the violence of my home life. But she could, and did, offer to let me stay with her for a week at a time during the summer.

She lived in a beautiful mansion in Mamaroneck, New York, that was surrounded by several acres of gardens and woodland. She may have stood only four feet, ten inches tall and weighed under a hundred pounds, but that didn't stop her from keeping the huge house clean and the gardens blooming. She taught me that hard work held many rewards, and that even when a job seemed insurmountable, all I had to do was keep at it until it was done.

Nana moved to California when I was six or seven, and I was devastated. Her house had been my haven. The most serious harm I'd experienced there was the old gray cat, George, drooling on me, or the orange striped cat, Murphy, kneading my pants leg with his claws.

After she moved away, I wrote to Nana and she always wrote back. She tried to send birthday and

Christmas presents, but my parents didn't allow us to observe any holidays.

When I went to college in Texas, Nana sent care packages of crisp, spiced cookies that kept for weeks and tasted wonderful. Her care packages were simple due to her limited income, but her determination to share with me taught me if I wanted to give, there would always be a way.

When I moved to Pasadena, California, Nana let my boyfriend and I stay with her for two weeks in her small apartment, though that meant I had to share her small bed, and my boyfriend had to sleep on her narrow couch. I don't remember thanking her when it was time for me to leave. She fed us without complaining about the price of food and took me clothes shopping. My aunt and uncle were often concerned that she overextended herself, but I think they understood why she took such great pleasure in being able to do things for me.

My relationship with Nana may sound pretty normal to someone from a loving family, but in my family, Nana was the foundation of my faith in humanity. Though I was raised in a fundamentalist Evangelical setting instead of the Catholic faith as she'd been, Nana never judged or preached at me. When my personal beliefs led me away from organized religion, she never pressured me about going to church with her. She knew that I believed in a compassionate God who was accessible to all, and in that, we could both agree.

She didn't drive, but she came with my aunt and uncle to my college graduation and told me she was proud of me.

That was only three years ago. How quickly the time had flown! I felt another shudder of grief pass through me, and I wished I'd told Nana more often how much her care had meant to me. I'd simply called her and told her what I needed, and she'd done her best to help me. Whether it was money for a semester at college or a place to stay, she did whatever she could to make it happen.

The morning after Liz had so kindly made spaghetti for me, I awoke to find a note lying beside my pillow. It was written in Liz's handwriting and said: "I found this prayer and thought it might help." I read the prayer once, then again, a slow smile spreading across my face as hope entered my heart. Yes, Liz, I thought, this is just what I needed to hear.

The prayer Liz had found reminded me of the faith that was at the core of my relationship with Nana. We had met as two souls with differing views on organized religion, but the same belief in goodness, mercy, and love. The prayer helped me remember that neither death nor God had taken Nana from me. She would live on in my heart as always. I realized I no longer needed the telephone to call my Nana, because, suddenly, she felt closer than she had when she was alive.

I held the note to my chest and stood looking through the yellow bedroom curtains into the bright morning. My gaze soared past the clouds, to a special place in the universe where I knew my Nana was watching. Holding the prayer against my heart with one hand and reaching toward her with the other, I said, "Thank you, Nana. Thank you."

~Kriss Erickson

The British Ambulance Driver

Majestic King, forever wise,
You melt my heart, which once was cold,
And when your beauty fills my eyes
It makes them young, which once were old.
Christ, my creator, hear my cry,
I am yours, you can I hear,
My Savior, Lover, yours am I,
My heart to yours be ever near.
Whether in life or death's last hour,
If sickness, pain or health you give,
Or shame, or honor, weakness, power,
Thankful is the life I live.

—Teresa of Avila

A web of tubes and monitors, whiffs of antiseptic stench, and a whirlwind of starched-and-sterile people had invaded my world. I lay there, drenched in a pool of tears, following emergency surgery and my first miscarriage. It was the darkest day of my twenty-two years.

A nurse burst into the room, laden with assorted instruments and carrying a clipboard. Without so much as a glance at my face, she began adjusting knobs and carrying out her duties, hardly aware or concerned that she was taking the pulse of a frightened girl whose world had just caved in.

"Where is my husband?" I choked back the tears and struggled to get up.

"No word from him." The nurse shrugged without skipping a beat, except to push me back down onto the pillow. "Just lie still."

None of us knew he had been involved in an accident and was being detained in a police station hundreds of kilometers away from this northern England hospital. Alone, scared, and confused, I tried to be brave, telling myself to "get a grip," but I was overcome by grief. My room was on the maternity ward and my sorrow was intensified by the sound of crying newborns. I was hours away from our tiny cottage and an ocean away from loved ones. Reality sent me searching for reason.

I cried out to God. "How could You let this happen?" It was more of a cold-hearted indictment than a candid inquiry. Momentary guilt for my outburst was quickly replaced by endless questions. Was God punishing me? Had I wanted a baby *too* much? Was I putting my desires for motherhood ahead of any devotion to Him? Did He know I was suffering? Did He care?

My heart *had* grown cold and indifferent through my college years. I had clothed myself in a shroud of self-sufficiency and hardly saw a need for God in my life. That was for the weak and needy; I was above all that. I bit my lip and tightened my grip on the bed rail.

"I'll get through this, I will." But then, in the next breath, a desperate plea, punctuated by muffled sobs. "Can you hear me, Lord? If you're there, I . . . I need You. I'm alone and sad. And so afraid. I don't think I can do this."

They wheeled me into a vacant room at the end of the hall, and in the stillness, my thoughts turned to the tragic events leading up to this moment. We had been so eager to spread the news about our baby, due in early May, that for the first time in my life, I had sent out my Christmas cards early. The day after I mailed the last card, it happened.

I had awakened at five with severe cramps and bleeding. I strained to reach the phone, and painstakingly dialed the number in my head for the Air Force alert shack, where my husband was pulling twenty-four-hour duty. "Something's happening," I said when he answered the phone. "I-I think I'm losing the baby!"

"I'll call the ambulance," he replied. "Don't move! Let them come upstairs to you."

Panic stricken, I stayed in bed, listening for the ambulance and waiting for what seemed like an eternity. The pain intensified. I gripped the mattress and held on. At last, the distant howl of the sirens grew closer, until the hush of night was pierced by an ominous, deafening sound, just below my window.

Then I remembered. I would have to leave the upstairs bed to unlock the downstairs door. I slowly rolled to the edge of the bed and slid to the floor. Doubled over with pain, I grabbed a sheet, wrapped it around me, and stumbled down the stairs toward the back door.

The persistent pounding didn't increase my speed, just my heart rate. I finally reached the door and stretched one arm up to unlatch the chain while clutching the sheet with the other. Still unable to stand up straight, I turned the knob slowly and opened the door.

Within seconds, I found myself nose to nose with a British ambulance driver, who had bent over to match my 90-degree angle. He tipped his hat and greeted me in a crisp English accent. "Oh, a jolly-good top-o-the-mornin' to ya, madam!" he said in a cheerful voice. "Are you the young lady who needed the ambulance?"

Later that night in hospital, I suddenly pictured the ambulance driver and myself bent over and his kind, yet rather obvious question. I began to chuckle. The more I thought about it, the more I laughed. Before I knew it, the depressing surroundings and tragedy of my loss were overshadowed by a wonderful sense of the ridiculous. God had brought a healing touch of levity into my lonely room.

In a peculiar, unexpected way, He had answered my prayer by sending laughter to help me cope, and to shine a glimmer of light through the gloomy darkness of my grief. A huge grin spread across my face as I looked up and whispered, "Thank You."

I could picture God smiling back. Only He knew the powerful impact a jovial ambulance driver and a lonely hospital room would have on a frightened girl who needed to get right with Him.

Eventually my husband arrived at the hospital, shaken but uninjured, and the following day, we made the journey back home to our cottage. I had already begun my journey back to God. In one momentous day, He had managed to lift my spirits, and wisely set me on a course that involved much-needed "heart surgery." Some of us have hearts that need to be tenderized first. Thankfully, that's His specialty.

A love relationship began to blossom between my Savior and me, unlike anything I had ever known.

Compelled to know Him more intimately, I took my Bible from the shelf and blew the dust from its cover. Inside, I discovered glorious nuggets of truth about the worth, the beauty, the wisdom, and the majesty of Christ. My shell of prideful self-sufficiency began to crumble—I had been humbled. I embraced His promises and thanked Him for His strength in my weakness, His love even in my unloveliness, and the comfort He had been longing to give me.

~Sandi Banks

God's Love Through Fire, Water, and Pain

*When I think of all this, I fall to my knees
and pray to the Father, the Creator of
everything in heaven and on earth. I pray
that from his glorious, unlimited resources
he will empower you with inner strength
through his Spirit. Then Christ will make
his home in your hearts as you trust in
him. Your roots will grow down into God's
love and keep you strong. And may you
have the power to understand, as all
God's people should, how wide, how long,
how high, and how deep his love is.*

—Ephesians 3:14–18

Humming and dancing to tunes on the radio,
I whipped up a salad and dessert to go with
the meat my husband, Thurman, was grilling. Glanc-
ing out the kitchen window, I could see my two-year-
old daughter, Amelia, toddling around her swing
set. She was being Daddy's helper by keeping him

company. It was a perfect day for our little family to enjoy a picnic.

I was standing over the stove when I heard my husband yell, "Evangeline, come quick. I need your help now!" The urgency in his voice made me drop my utensils and run to the window. Replacing the peaceful picture I had witnessed seconds before was a scene of horror. Our large backyard had become a sea of fire, and Amelia was trapped in the middle with flames licking around her chubby bare legs!

By the time I rushed outside, Thurman had run through the flames, scooped up Amelia, and tossed her over by the fence, out of harm's way. I gingerly took little Mia into my arms, carried her inside, and headed straight for our favorite blue rocking chair. I began to rock and sing, but my intense fear wouldn't allow me to check her body for burns, so I started to pray.

For me, times of extreme fear have been similar to descriptions I've heard about near-death experiences. Even as I prayed and sang, past experiences ran through my mind, especially the memory of my brush with death in the Kansas City Flood of 1977. I was seventeen and driving in a blinding rainstorm from my job at a modeling agency to a meeting on the famous downtown Plaza.

As the rains became stronger and more violent,

God led me to change directions and head toward home. The heavy waterfall on my windshield soon obstructed my vision, and my car began floating, so that I could no longer steer. Eventually, a policeman rescued me from my stalled vehicle and arranged for my car to be towed to safety. On the ride home, he told me that a family had drowned in their car three blocks away. A total of thirty people drowned in the Plaza area.

Remembering God's faithfulness gave me the courage to check for injury to Mia's legs. They were not black from smoke, and there were no burns. The only sign of her fiery encounter was the fact that all the fine, silky hairs on her legs were curled into tiny circles. With tears of gratitude and joy, I began to sing an old hymn I had sung in church as a child, called "God Leads His Dear Children Along." The chorus of the song was particularly meaningful to me. "Some through the waters, some through the floods, some through the fire . . . but God gives a song in the night season and all the day long."

I also recalled a Bible verse I learned long ago in vacation Bible school. Romans 8:35 (NLT) reads, "Can anything ever separate us from Christ's love? Does it mean he no longer loves us if we have trouble or calamity, or are persecuted, or hungry, or destitute, or in danger, or threatened with death?"

God may not protect us from problems, harm, or pain, but He promises to be with us and love us in all situations.

About ten years after the scare with my older daughter, Amelia, my faith was to be tested—not once, but twice—with my younger daughter, Lydia. One day, when Lydia was two years old, she was in child care at a health club where I was swimming laps. She ended up in a hallway by the racquet-ball courts, and there, someone slammed a door and cut off a third of her pinkie finger. An ambulance rushed us to a hospital, and a specialist attempted to surgically reattach the rest of her finger, but it fell off weeks later.

Somehow, with much prayer, we survived that trauma. Lydia had to relearn everything she had done with her right hand because it had been bandaged for so long. I had almost stopped thinking about the accident every day when we were hit by another challenge. At age three, Lydia fell victim to a sexual assault by a family friend at church. The police, doctors, psychologists, and detectives became our new best friends as we worked diligently to help her in every conceivable way.

Once again, Lydia seemed to heal. She remained a happy little girl, surrounded by love, but I was struggling. The questions that couldn't be answered plagued my waking hours and evolved into nightmares. My prayers became one-sided diatribes aimed somewhere in God's direction. "Why have you protected me so many times throughout my life? Why did you deliver Amelia from harm, and then choose not to take care of Lydia? What's that all about? She was just a toddler, so what great important lesson is she supposed to be learning from all her suffering?"

I'm not sure what kept me praying and reading my Bible. I was so angry and so confused, but I had grown up with a preacher for a daddy. I kept doing all the Christian "stuff" because I was pretty sure that I wouldn't find peace anywhere else. As a desperate woman, I kept searching for reasons and meaning. As a mom, I felt that I owed it to Lydia to persevere in presenting her case to heaven. I had to work out my faith in God, so I could tell her with sincerity and conviction that God was a loving Father and worthy of her trust.

At some point in my journey over the past seven years, I returned to my favorite chapter in the Bible—Romans 8. The twenty-eighth verse (NLT) says, "And we know that God causes everything to work together for the good of those who love God and are called according to his purpose for them." I couldn't argue with that. By the time Lydia was four, I could see that she had been blessed with a miraculous gift of compassion and wisdom beyond her years. The mothers of Lydia's playmates and her teachers constantly commented on how extraordinary she was. Time after time, I saw God's hand on Lydia and saw His Spirit at work in her.

Exhausted by my constant anger and agitation, I finally decided to call it even. If God was going to be abundantly gracious to Lydia now, I would give up my outrage over the past. With a renewed sense of peace in my heart, I was able to see how God had used the times of difficulty to build our faith. Our family began to experience His abundant blessings and the vastness of His love in almost every area of our lives. Just as Paul promised in Romans 8:37 (NLT), God was proving to me that in all circumstances, "overwhelming victory is ours through Christ, who loved us."

Now ten, Lydia boldly shares her testimony of God's love. At a Thanksgiving church service, she stood before two hundred people and talked about her faith. She sings solos at church and school with great joy because God has revealed His love to her in such a powerful way. Who am I to question the ways of God? I continue to pray that I will mature in my faith. Only then will I begin to understand the awesome and infinite love of the God I serve.

~Evangeline Beals Gardner

Oh, Lucy!

*O merciful God, fill our hearts with the
graces of your Holy Spirit—with love, joy,
peace, long-suffering, gentleness, goodness, faith, humbleness, self-control.
Teach us to love those who hate us, to pray
for those who despitefully use us so that we
may be your children, our Father, who make
your sun to shine on the evil and on the good
and send rain on the just and on the unjust.*

—Anselm of Canterbury

It's been over three years since my husband sold
Lucy a red Pontiac Grand Am. Nice car—really
sharp—and he gave her a great deal, too. That's
what my husband does, buys and fixes and sells cars.
He can fix anything.

Lucy is retired, and divorced, and she's, well, difficult. She's a lonely woman, and if you show the
least civility in listening to her, she never quits. We
have heard the entire story of her dysfunctional family, her complete health history, and all about every

car she's ever owned and everything that ever went wrong with them. Lucy can go on and on and on. We've tried to share our faith with her, but Lucy's specialty is talking, not listening.

When she calls, my heart sinks because I know she's having a problem with her car. She'll ask Jim to fix it, and he will, and, somehow, she never pays. What a deal to buy a used car that comes with a lifetime of absolutely free service.

The problem is, Lucy makes us put our money, along with our Christianity, where our mouths are. We can say we'd do unto others as we'd have them do unto us, but with Lucy, we can't get away with just saying it. We have to do it. And she seems so ungrateful. I find my faith continually challenged.

You see, we take our faith seriously. We read the Bible and attempt to live by what we read. We consider Christianity a way of life rather than a religion. Lucy challenges me because I see her using my husband and I'd do anything to defend him. So I complain bitterly. "No one expects you to give so sacrificially. She is taking advantage of you. This is your livelihood—you have to charge her!" On and on, and all my gripes are quite legitimate.

Everyone agrees it's gone too far. "Now you are just enabling her to take advantage and rewarding her irresponsibility," they say. Oh, yes, my friends and family completely validate my pouting attitude.

Once, she'd been told her brakes needed work, but she ignored the advice. Then she called Jim. Now, because of her neglect, a relatively easy and inexpensive job had turned into one that required much more work, time, and expense. And Jim did it. Then he called Lucy.

She asked if we could return the car.

Sure, Lucy, no problem. We deliver. I sputtered all the way. She had asked Jim what he had spent on parts, and he told her $35 would cover it. Not only did he drop the price considerably, he didn't even take his own time into account. When we got to her place, Lucy was not there. We've never seen that $35.

When Lucy calls, it's always an emergency. Always. She's demanding and inconsiderate. How do you deal with someone like that? I pray, "Lord, help me see Lucy through your eyes, to love her, and not resent helping her, but to see an opportunity to do something to please you."

Lucy moved about two hours away. Whew. But whenever she's in town, she'll call, needing something or other looked at or fixed on that car. Most of the problems are her own fault, like when she backed over a curb and ripped out the exhaust. "Could you fix it before tomorrow?" Just exasperating.

I have no trouble admitting that I don't like Lucy. Anyone who takes advantage of my husband and fails to appreciate his generosity gets no courtesy from me. I'd just as soon hang up on her. Not only is she unappreciative of Jim's efforts, he is less than appreciative of my attempts to protect him from her abuses.

He considers what he does for Lucy a ministry. He reminds me that she is on a fixed income and probably can't afford to pay. I point out that our bills have to be paid, too, and that his time is money, after all. Jim tells me my attitude is wrong, that giving to Lucy is like lending to the Lord, and He promises to repay. This makes me like Lucy even less. Jim and I rarely argue, but whenever she calls, this conversation is repeated. It makes me angry because it points out my weak faith and immaturity, and I don't like the accompanying shame. Dealing with Lucy is miserable for me, but I've come to recognize that the discomfort is akin to growing pains.

Recently, we were having a perfectly wonderful week. We'd bought copies of Eugene Peterson's New Testament paraphrase, *The Message*, and were enjoying deep and meaningful fellowship as we daily read the Scriptures together. We were frequently moved by the power and relevance of God's word.

Then Lucy called.

Of course, she was having a crisis. It was a bitterly cold morning, and we hadn't even had our time in the Word yet. She was calling from a wrecker. Her car had quit running, and she just had to have it right away to get back home. Her cat had been alone for days and she was frantic. On and on she went, using the wrecker driver's phone. Jim's attempt to diagnose the problem fell on Lucy's deaf ears, so that the part of the conversation I heard sounded like, "Is it . . . Did you . . . Has it . . . Where . . . ?" Finally—of course—Jim told her that she could have the car brought here, and he would see what he could do. She told him she'd call in an hour. Jim said she'd better wait for two because he wouldn't even have time to look at it, let alone fix it, in one hour.

I lost it. How dare she presume he had nothing else to do but wait on her? Why didn't he just tell her to get someone else to deal with it? Why did he think he owed her anything? How many times was he going to coddle her selfish behavior and give up time and money for someone who didn't even appreciate it? And by the way, there was that $35 she still owed us.

"Don't you think I know that?" Jim said. "It would sure be easier to pass this off and get rid of her, but that doesn't seem Christlike. I don't enjoy dealing with Lucy, but she keeps coming into my life, so my goal is to fix that car without muttering or complaining, as if I really was doing it for Jesus. I'm trying to trust God here."

I pouted.

Jim told me kindly that I needed to repent, that my attitude was wrong, that this was an opportunity to act like Jesus and that, after all, Jesus didn't wait for me to be nice to him before he *died* for me. Jim was right, and his words devastated me. I was only trying to protect him, wasn't I?

The wrecker brought the car, and Jim put it in his shop and started a fire to warm it up. I resigned myself to the fact that, once again, Lucy would get her way. I tried to pray and get my attitude in agreement with what I profess to believe. While the car thawed out, we opened *The Message*. We'd been working our way through the Epistles. The bookmark was in Romans, at the beginning of chapter fifteen, and I began to read aloud.

"Those of us who are strong and able in the faith need to step in and lend a hand to those who falter, and not just do what is most convenient for us."

The words startled me and tears sprang to my eyes. "Okay, God. Point taken," I said, attempting to be flip about it, but His word had nailed me, and I was undone. I wiped my eyes and continued.

"Strength is for service, not status. Each one of us needs to look after the good of the people around us, asking ourselves, 'How can I help?' That's exactly what Jesus did. He didn't make it easy for himself by avoiding people's troubles but waded right in and helped out."

By now, I was so convicted and so blessed by God's nurturing, I could barely see. We were both weeping for joy at God's perfect care and encouragement. We laughed and cried, praising God for his word.

I floated through that day, acutely aware of my Heavenly Father's love for me. He did not let me stay in that pouting, immature attitude, but dealt lovingly with me, using his word to guide me carefully, yet firmly, back to the path that leads to life. I knew with certainty that I was His child, and that He was intimately involved in my life.

And once it got warmed up, Lucy's car was fine. She had only flooded it.

~Dianne Meredith Vogel

Protecting the Nest

Give us, O Lord, a steadfast heart, which
no unworthy affection may drag down-
wards; give us an unconquered heart, which
no tribulation can wear out; give us an
upright heart, which no unworthy purpose
may tempt aside. Bestow upon us also, O
Lord our God, understanding to know you,
diligence to seek you, wisdom to find you,
and a faithfulness that may finally embrace
you; through Jesus Christ our Lord.

— *St. Thomas Aquinas*

We all gathered in the living room. It had been a long, hot day, and I wasn't sure I wanted to hear what our youngest daughter, Amanda, had to say. I doubted my husband, Gary, was in any mood for conversation, either.

"I have something to tell you," said Amanda, in a quiet, timid voice.

My astute husband blurted out, "You're pregnant!"

"Yes," she said. This was not good news. It meant

she was about to graduate from high school with a baby growing inside her.

The first words out of my mouth were, "Do you want to get married?"

She shook her head emphatically. "No!"

The word spilled out of Gary's mouth. "Abortion?" he asked. Even though we didn't approve of abortion, I caught myself thinking it might be a good idea. Our proud hearts were being tempted to go against God and His Word. It had been easy to trust Him in the good times. Would we remain faithful to Him through this tough situation, or would we miss the great blessing He must have in store for us? Fortunately, the decision was taken out of our hands.

Amanda's answer was quick and determined. "It's too late for an abortion. I'm already four months pregnant. I want this baby very badly, and it has nothing to do with you!"

I could see the anger in Gary's eyes, but I knew his heart must be breaking, just as mine was. "Father God," I prayed, "forgive us for even thinking about abortion. Give us the grace to be patient with Amanda, the mercy to let our anger go, and the wisdom to handle this situation as You would have us do. In Your precious Son's name. Amen."

As the days went by, moving us closer to the birth of our first grandchild, I reminisced about the early days of our marriage, when Gary and I were having our children. Before I became pregnant with Amanda, I asked God to give us a boy. I thought a boy would complement our two girls nicely. Our family would be perfect—a typical American family.

I had a hard time getting pregnant, but I continued to pray for a boy. It had been so easy the first two times; I couldn't understand the delay. As I persisted in my petitions for our third child, God spoke to my heart. "I have something better in store for you," He said. "Will you accept My gift whether it is a boy or a girl?"

"Yes," I said willingly. I became pregnant shortly afterward.

When our third daughter, Amanda Faith, arrived, I knew she was our pearl of great price. What a good baby and what a happy child she was! She and I were very close, but as she approached her teenage years, we seemed to be always disagreeing. She thought I was clueless about what really went on in the world. I thought she was rejecting everything we stood for as a Christian family. We saw the world from two different points of view. Then, she became pregnant.

Amanda presented us with a beautiful seven-pound, six-ounce baby boy. She lay in her hospital bed, clutching her tight-eyed newborn with a smug but scared look on her face. The baby, whom

Amanda named Kaleel, was our first grandchild and our first boy. Was this the "son" I had prayed for so many years ago? What would this child mean in our lives? What would God teach us as we watched this little boy grow? Would he grow to know, love, and trust God? Without an earthly father, He would surely need a Heavenly Father.

We arranged things so Amanda and Kaleel could live with us. Amanda went to cosmetology school every day, and I proceeded to raise her son. He captured my heart immediately, and Gary fondly nicknamed Kaleel his "Bubba Boy." I prayed that Amanda would draw closer to God. I prayed for her to take more responsibility for Kaleel's care. I prayed that Kaleel would feel loved and cherished by his mother. I prayed for a father for our grandson. And I prayed for continued steadfastness as Gary and I waited on the Lord.

Amanda and Kaleel moved into low-cost, government housing when Kaleel was two and a half. As he grew older, Kaleel realized the other boys had dads and he didn't. Amanda began to date, always keeping in mind that her little one needed a good father. It was hard to find someone willing to take on an instant family. It made us sad to see our daughter and grandson so unsettled.

When Kaleel was six years old, Amanda met

Keith. He was the Herculean type, well built, with broad shoulders. His longish blond hair and clear blue eyes softened his soldierlike demeanor. He was always respectful and treated our daughter and grandson with great kindness.

As Amanda and Keith dated, Kaleel became more and more attached to Keith. One day, Kaleel begged me, "If Keith asks Grandpop if he can marry my mommy, tell him to say, 'Yes'" More time went by, but I didn't see them making any progress toward marriage. Keith had some bad memories that needed healing first.

In spite of this, Keith taught Amanda how to discipline Kaleel and how to take more responsibility as a mother. He was a great influence on our grandson and seemed to genuinely care about him. I began praying that Keith would either ask Amanda to marry him, or that they would break up before one of them got hurt. "Lord," I prayed, "please enable Keith to give his love away without fear of suffering. Teach him about your unconditional love—how wide and long and high and deep it is. Encourage him to put his trust in You, knowing You will keep his heart safe in the palm of Your hand."

As I prayed, I pictured an eagle, wings outstretched over a nest, protecting its young. I was familiar with the Old Testament symbol of God as an eagle. It seemed as if God was showing me He would cover Amanda, Keith, and Kaleel with His great power and love. I believed without a doubt God was in charge of this family. He had everything under control. I knew God would teach them how to love each other with a love that could not be broken.

Months turned into years, as we steadfastly continued to wait on the Lord. Then one day, Keith called Gary on the phone. By this time, Kaleel was approaching his ninth birthday. With a nervous laugh, Keith finally asked, "May I have your permission to marry Amanda?" I had told Gary years ago about Kaleel's desperate plea for Gary to give his permission, but that day, he didn't need any encouragement. He gave Keith his blessing.

During their one-year engagement, Kaleel asked his mom the same question over and over. "When can I call Keith 'Dad'?" Amanda kept putting him off, not sure if Keith was ready to be addressed that way.

As their wedding day approached, I pleaded with God to soften Keith's heart and make him tender, receptive, and responsive to Kaleel's love. I asked God to show him how much Kaleel needed him.

The wedding took place on a brisk autumn day. Almost ten years old, Kaleel was the junior best man. On his wrist he wore a brand-new ID bracelet. The night before, at the rehearsal dinner, Amanda and Keith gave him a present. Kaleel opened it, took one look at the bracelet, and ran across the room to Keith. He put his arms around Keith's waist and buried his head in Keith's chest. At first, Keith stood, arms at his side, unsure of what to do.

Kaleel did not let go of Keith. All eyes were on them, and the only sound in the room was Kaleel's quiet sobs. Slowly, very slowly, Keith put one arm around Kaleel, and then the other. The two of them clung to each other for about ten minutes. Later, when I looked at the bracelet through my own tears, I saw the words engraved on it. It read, "To Kaleel. Love, Mom and Dad." Our grandson, our Bubba son, had found an earthly father.

Amanda and Keith have been married for almost three years. I see many growing pains, but God is still protecting their nest. He is faithfully showing them what His love can do in their lives. He is granting them understanding to know Him, diligence to seek Him, wisdom to find Him, and a faithfulness that may finally embrace Him as their heavenly Father.

Does God answer the prayers of a steadfast heart? You bet He does! And with His answers come great blessings beyond our wildest imaginations.

~Mercedes B. Evans

Finding Grace
in God's Sight

This same God who takes care of me
will supply all your needs from his glorious
riches, which have been given to us in
Christ Jesus. Now glory be to God our
Father forever and ever. Amen.

—*Philippians 4:19–20*

Being a practical kid, I took something I liked to do—writing—and figured out how to get paid for doing it. After graduating, I got a job in corporate public relations, writing stories about everything from an employee with a pet python to the company's role in the space program.

What a great job! Every word I wrote was paid for! Every story I wrote was published! How many writers could say that? When friends complained about job-related stress, I couldn't relate to their difficulties. *This is work?* I thought. *I should be paying them to let me do it.*

Things changed in the mid-eighties. My company

started "belt-tightening," "process re-engineering," and "downsizing." The axe fell daily. Rumors swirled. People started watching their backs. My boss, afraid of his boss, made me rewrite things again and again. His boss, afraid of her boss, sent the rewrite machine into overdrive. Soon I was doing more second-guessing than writing.

One assignment landed on my desk at 6:00 P.M. I stayed up all night, writing and deleting, writing and deleting, "perfecting" the piece to within an inch of its life. The next morning, when I handed it in, I felt as if I'd run a marathon: exhausted but exhilarated for actually crossing the finish line.

The exhilaration didn't last. My boss read the piece, scrunched up her face, and stared at the ceiling. "It needs something," she said. "I don't know what, but I'll know it when I see it."

If *she* didn't know what she wanted, how was *I* supposed to?

Then I was assigned to write a speech for the company president. I didn't write for Ted very often; that was my boss's job. I was more than a little nervous when I took the speech to his office for review.

Ted must have sensed my unease. He welcomed me, came out from behind his desk, and gestured toward a cluster of comfy chairs. Did I want coffee? "No thanks."

My hands were shaking too much to hold a cup.

"I understand you've got something for me to read," he said pleasantly. I handed him a copy of the speech. He smiled and looked down at the manuscript. Immediately, his eyes bounced off the page and focused on mine. "The first line," he said. "I don't like it."

I read the offending sentence: "Hello, I'm Ted Brown." Thinking he was joking, I added, "You *are* Ted Brown, aren't you?"

"Yeeesssss," he replied. "I am. I just don't like that line."

If he didn't like, "Hello, I'm Ted Brown," I was in trouble. That's when I started losing confidence. If I couldn't even write the opening line of a speech, what *could* I write?

I developed writer's block. Sunrise and sunset found me staring at the same blank computer screen. For every five words I wrote, I deleted four. I locked myself in my office where no one could "get me." I hated my job. I hated myself.

My friends sympathized. At Mari's suggestion, I took writing courses. "Try writing with your computer monitor turned off," one instructor said. "That way, you can't edit yourself. You'll write freely. Your writer's block will be cured." When I tried this technique, I ended up with a screen full of "Noe id yhr yimr got sll hoof mrn yo vomr yo yhr sif og yhrit vounyty."

Vicki shared articles about writer's block. One said, "Write at the same time every day," which wasn't helpful since I couldn't write at *any* time of day. Another article asked, "Whose voice do you hear inside your head, criticizing you? Your parents? Your first-grade teacher? Your ex-husband?" This is deep, I thought. So I tried therapy.

Then my friends' advice took a spiritual turn. Ed, my lawn-mowing guy, loaned me a book on creativity that said things like:

"God has no hands but yours with which to work, no voice but yours with which to speak."

"Work is a form of prayer; it glorifies God."

"Skills and abilities are God-given. It's not up to you whether to use them or not."

Next, while handing me a prescription for antidepressants, my doctor asked if I went to church. When I said no, I really didn't *believe*, he suggested going to the planetarium. "It's a spiritual experience," he said. "It will give you perspective."

Then my friend Carol, a Christian counselor, suggested prayer. "Give the problem up to God," she said. "Ask Him to remove all roadblocks. Put Him in the driver's seat."

I tried the exercises in Ed's book; visited the planetarium, which *was* a spiritual experience; and went to church for the first time in thirty years. And

I started praying, even though it didn't seem right to ask for help with writer's block while God was dealing with wars, poverty, and disease. But Ed's book reassured me. "God's power and love are boundless. There's plenty for everyone."

Carol also recommended Exodus 33:12–17. I didn't relate to it at first. But with repeated reading, it became clearer and clearer. That's when things began to turn around for me.

In Exodus 33, the Israelites build a golden calf. Frustrated and angry, Moses questions his ability to lead them to the Promised Land. He confronts God. "*You* asked me to lead these people," he complains, "but you haven't given me any help."

Moses's work was, literally, the Lord's work. But he didn't feel competent to do it, despite his God-given leadership ability, charisma, intelligence, and courage—not to mention desert-survival skills. Moses ignored the fact that, out of all the people on earth, God gave him the job, along with the natural ability and worldly experience he needed to carry it out.

This made me think: God had blessed me with a news-writer father, a grammar-and-composition-obsessed grade-school principal, a journalism degree, and a love of my craft. God had chosen me, out of all others, to be in my particular job, with my particular coworkers, and with my own set of business challenges. Then I thought, maybe writing for a big company wasn't my real job after all.

Maybe God placed me here to mentor young writers; to instruct, entertain, and uplift with my words; to be a loving, caring colleague; and to stay up all night to get my boss out of a jam. I realized that every time I stared at a blank screen, unable to write, I was dismissing my God-given abilities and rejecting God's assignment.

In Exodus, God reassures Moses, "You have found grace in my sight, and I know you by name." God knew Moses before he was in his mother's womb. Of course he knew that Moses was the man for the job.

Now that I'm a practicing Christian, I'm confident that I have found grace in God's sight and that He knows me by name. One day He'll ask for an accounting of my job performance and how well I made use of the tools He gave me. With faith and a grateful heart, I hope to earn a good appraisal.

Today I enjoy my work—my God-given work—and take pleasure in letting God's creativity flow through me. Like Moses, I ask for and experience God's presence. Every morning, I reread Exodus 33:14–17. And I pray.

~Patricia Bridgman

Building a Bridge
to Heaven

Make a joyful noise unto the
Lord, all ye lands.
Serve the Lord with gladness;
come before his presence with singing.
Know ye that the Lord he is God;
it is he that hath made us,
and not we ourselves;
we are his people, and the sheep of his pasture.
Enter into his gates with thanksgiving,
and into his courts with praise;
be thankful unto him, and bless his name.
For the Lord is good; his mercy is everlasting;
and his truth endureth to all generations.

—Psalm 100

My first grandchild, three-year-old Katie, leaned forward in her car seat and craned her neck so as to catch my eye. "Grandmamma, what are you saying?" she asked.

I was wedged in the center lane of traffic,

trying to see the car in front of me. Heavy sheets of rain washed across the windshield while the wipers worked double time. Eighteen-wheelers passed on both sides of me, throwing up tidal waves, making it hard to see the signs ahead. I was afraid I would be unable to see my highway connection and would miss it. So I was secretly praying with my eyes wide open, not realizing that my lips were moving. Katie's innocent little voice relaxed my stern face, and I smiled. "I'm praying, Katie. Praying that God will get us safely through this storm."

Fifteen years later, my Katie is on her way to college, and I'm still praying for God to take her safely through this life. The prayers that began when she was being formed in her mother's womb are endless, and most of my prayers for her; her sister, Molly; and her brother, Pete, are spoken silently for only God to hear.

Someday soon, I'll tell my first grandchild everything I've learned in my sixty-something years about prayer—the greatest link we have from this earth to heaven. It is the connection Jesus modeled for us when he got up early and went out to a lonely place to pray and receive direction from His heavenly Father.

Perhaps I'll say, "Katie, I think the habit of prayer gets passed down from one generation to another.

I watched your Gran-Gran on her knees many times, her mouth moving quietly. She prayed about everything; nothing was too big or too small to talk to God about. I believe that God was just as real to Mom in her bedroom or at the breakfast table as He was in church.

"As a divorced parent, Mom was wholly responsible for her children's welfare. The task was too big for one woman, but her parents had taught her to turn to God. I know that her petitions kept me, her rebellious teenage daughter, from disaster. Her prayers also brought your great-uncle Wayne out of a jungle in Vietnam, spared his life when a bullet came within an inch of his heart, and brought him from alcoholism to sobriety.

I watched my mom pray, and I went with her to church. I saw God as someone in the distant sky, someone to be respected, for sure, but I prayed only when I was in trouble. Even then, I wondered if God was really listening. Nevertheless, Mom's quiet prayers were like a slow marinating process that eventually drew me into a closer relationship with her God. After I married your granddad and we experienced the blessing of your dad's birth, we eagerly searched for heavenly help. What a responsibility we had! There were no parenting classes back then, and we made so many mistakes. I suspect that prayer was the only useful thing we knew how to do when we were young parents.

"Because of your Gran-Gran's prayers for me, I came to believe there was an unseen world around us, inhabited by angels sent by God to both protect me and nudge me. Sometimes the angels closed doors I wasn't meant to enter; sometimes they opened doors and escorted me safely along the pathway that God planned for me. I have always believed that their help in my life was the direct result of prayer, and it's prayer that builds a bridge to heaven, a bridge that ends with God, holding the gate wide open.

Sometimes the bridge was hard to build; my ability to pray overcome by the dark times in my life. Sometimes it took more than a casual Sunday prayer to achieve a miracle; seasons of fasting were necessary, when I hunkered down and stayed on my knees. At times, I prayed without ceasing, and I still didn't see God working or feel His presence. But, as with the Christmas cactus that needs a season away from the light, something grew in the darkness—something that bloomed in God's time.

"Katie, you must never forget that Halloween night when your dad, Uncle Rick, Granddad, and I had the automobile accident. We had been to a football game and were traveling home in the middle of the night. We all fell asleep, even Granddad, who was driving. I woke to the sound of Rick's voice, "Dad, wake up!" he shouted. The car was completely out of control, and we were swinging back and forth across the highway. We rocked and swerved off the road, then toppled over and over again; steel ground against steel as our bodies bounced and slammed with each jolt. In the midst of it, I remember thinking that we had prayed about this trip. We had even prayed for safe travel before leaving the gas station. Didn't God hear our prayers? I wanted to cry out, 'God, where are you now?' Although I tried to think of Scripture to pray, my brain was in shock, so I began mumbling, 'Jesus, Jesus, Jesus!'

"When we finally crashed into the ditch, three of us were sitting upright, still in seat belts. The dome light was shining overhead, enabling people on the highway to spot us in the darkness. But your dad was no longer in the backseat. He lay still on the ground, and we didn't know how he had gotten out of the car or if he was alive. At that moment I felt that God had abandoned us. And then someone called out of the darkness, 'Are you all right?' the voice asked. Medical students, who had been in the car behind us, came to our aid and called an ambulance.

"Later, we realized that your dad had been thrown out of the SUV through the window. Although there were shards of glass in his pockets, he had no cuts on his body, and he walked out of the hospital emergency room that night alive and well. What a miracle! But while that miracle had been in progress, it felt like disaster. When I thought God had forgotten us, He was busy dispatching angels to save our lives. God's work is like that; it is sometimes hidden in the darkest night.

"Katie, when you were three years old, your family could control so much of your life. But now we can't fasten you into the seat belt anymore, and take you where we want you to go. You are the driver now. You have a good foundation of faith, and you've been trained in the way you should go. So, we pray that you will build your own bridges to heaven now. We ask God to take you safely through all the storms, to send angels to guide you, and to open the highways that you should travel. And most of all, we pray you will know that your heavenly Father is always with you, even on the darkest night."

~*Virginia Dawkins*

The Young Man

In mercy you have seen fit to show me,
poor as I am, how we can in no way pass
judgment on other people's intentions.
Indeed, by sending people along an endless
variety of paths, you give me an example
of myself, and for this I thank you.

—Catherine of Siena

On a crisp November Wednesday, the faithful few had gathered to pray. Some kneeled at the altar, while others walked and prayed. Karen observed that it was a larger group than normal. The saints were deep into the prayer time, when the door creaked open and in he walked.

Karen glanced toward the door, just a few feet away. Her eyes took in the weathered face. Lines and bags told the unspoken story of a difficult life. Tears filled his bloodshot eyes as he scanned the room. Nervously, he brushed a dirty hand through a full head of greasy hair. His clothes were torn and filthy. The stench of body odor and cigarette smoke accosted her nostrils. She flinched and was tempted to move away, but something inside told her to stay. Others either didn't hear that still small voice or ignored it, as they cast disgusted looks toward the young man, and then moved quickly away.

The young man shuffled to the altar and fell to his knees and began to weep. Karen watched as his body shook, as years of emotion flowed in the form of tears. She wondered what huge burdens he carried. Which of life's struggles he faced. Everything in her screamed to walk away, but she was drawn to the young man. She placed a hand on his shoulder. He flinched. Another hand joined hers, then another, and another. Others watched with disdain.

Karen was saddened by the looks and actions of some in the room. They were probably concerned that he would stain the beautiful carpet or the fabric of the pew. Perhaps they were thinking that people like him belonged at the mission with those of his kind. Obviously, they didn't feel he fit at the church. She sensed the heart of the Lord breaking and felt His tears on her cheeks.

One among the group asked how they could pray for the young man. His history of childhood abuse, alcoholism, drugs, homelessness, and time in jail for child abuse rushed from his quivering lips. Tears flowed, coursing down his dirt-smudged cheeks like tributaries. Karen noticed the disgusted looks and heard the angry muttering: "A child abuser . . . a registered sex offender . . . he shouldn't be here . . . there are children in this church." The young man continued, describing his feelings of hopelessness and thoughts of suicide. A mother of five, Karen's heart broke for the hurting boy inside the damaged man. Her hand still upon his shoulder, she prayed silently, while others prayed aloud.

The door creaked open again, and a woman Karen knew slipped quietly into the sanctuary. She left the young man to greet her friend. They embraced and spoke quietly for a few minutes. Karen glanced back to the altar to see the huddled form still quaking, as two men prayed fervently for the young man. Compassion overwhelmed her, as she thought about him committing suicide because of loneliness. Instantly, the answer was clear. She would invite him to Thanksgiving at her home. No, that wasn't possible; she had young children at home. Yes, the Lord wanted her to invite this dirty, greasy, smelly young man to her home to celebrate Thanksgiving. No, what would her husband think? Her children? Karen, deeply entrenched in a spiritual battle, didn't notice the young man slip out.

Her heart ached as she scanned the hallways.

She had to find him. Outside, she saw a person ride off on a bicycle and ran for her van. Lord, if you lead me to him, I'll invite him, she whispered, half hoping she wouldn't find him. Looking down each side street, she was about to give up, when she saw him a couple of blocks away. She raced up next to him, rolled down the window, and asked him to stop. Fear quickly replaced compassion. There she was on an isolated street, getting out of the safety of her van to talk with a registered sex offender, yet the fear was quickly replaced by peace and a sense of protection.

The young man greeted her with a warm smile, as he recognized her from the church. They spoke long enough for Karen to get his name, the phone number of the place he was staying, and to invite him to Thanksgiving dinner. His face lit up like a child's on Christmas morning. He thanked her and rode off. It felt good, but now she had to face her husband and children with the idea.

At first, Karen's family wasn't too hot on the idea of having the man to their home, but they were soon convinced it was the right thing to do, so all was set. It was the right thing to do, wasn't it? she wondered. After all, Jesus had said to take care of the poor, hungry, and homeless. He told us that what we did to the least of these, we did to Him. A thought tickled her mind—what if Jesus visited the earth to test human kindness; perhaps he would come back as a dirty, smelly young man. Truly, what was done unto that man would be done unto Jesus. She wept at the thought of all those who had rejected him.

Several days passed, and Karen's heart was filled with joy. She had been walking with the Lord for only a few years, and this was her first time to reach out to someone who was truly hurting. She looked forward to Thanksgiving more than usual. That was until the phone call from the young man's parole officer, who read Karen the riot act about inviting a registered sex offender into a home full of children. She was told, in no uncertain terms, that the young man would not be coming for Thanksgiving dinner. Setting the receiver down, she wept and prayed, as she now had to call him.

He was angry, not with Karen, but at the system that had let him down and then condemned him to a life of shame. A bitter torrent of words flowed through the phone, bruising her spirit. Tears streaked her face as she replaced the receiver, her heart broken.

Karen stayed in touch with the young man and each week she saw him at church. One day, the phone rang and she recognized his excited voice. He had been released and could come over to the house anytime he was invited. After a discussion with her husband, they invited him for Christmas Day.

The young man became a part of the family, even calling Karen and her husband "Mom" and "Dad." He attended the many family functions—birthdays, Thanksgiving, Christmas, Easter, and the annual Fourth of July picnic. Each May, they would take the young man out to dinner for his birthday and play some sort of embarrassing prank. Although he complained, it was easy to see that those moments were among the most special in his entire life, as his own family had rejected him years earlier.

After living in spare rooms, small trailers, garages, and on the street, the young man found a nice Christian group home that greeted him with open arms. Following numerous bad experiences at church, he joined Karen and her husband at the church they had helped start. Finally, planted in a loving home and church, the young man began to grow and blossom.

He had dropped out of school at an early age and was often labeled stupid, but now he was taking classes at the church and thriving. He showered more often, groomed his hair, shaved, and wore nicer clothes. A servant's heart was very apparent in his willingness to do anything at the church. Soon he was asked to serve on the men's ministry committee, and following that, was given a key position at a Promise Keepers conference. The music pastor approached him and asked if he would join the worship team.

Today, the young man is serving God with his whole heart. He works full-time at the group home and has become a vital part of an operation that serves so many who are down and out. He has been honored numerous times at church, as the volunteer of the month. The anger and bitterness are gone. He is truly a new creation in Christ.

Michael is the young man's name. How appropriate that he would be named after the most powerful archangel, because he is now a powerful force for God. What Satan meant for evil, God turned to good.

Karen often thinks about that day, eleven years ago, when Michael walked in the door. She was tempted to react the same way as others, judging him by his appearance, and later, because of the mistakes he had made. She thanks God often for the strength it took to reach out to him and embrace him as a son.

Karen is my wife and Michael is our spiritual son. We love him as if he were one of our birth children, because we know, as with our other children, that Michael is a wonderful gift from God.

~Rod Nichols

Comfort in the
Questions of a Child

*May Jesus Christ, the King of glory, help
us to make the right use of all the suffering that comes to us and to offer to him the
incense of a patient and trustful heart.*

—Johannes Tauler

I opened my wallet to pay my son Dennis for tend-
ing his little sisters, and a picture fell out. I pulled
out $10 while Dennis picked the picture up from the
floor. He regarded it, absently taking the money from
my hand.

"Is that a picture of Keena's funeral?" he asked.

"Yes, it is," I said.

Together we looked at the small pink coffin, covered with white carnations and red roses. I felt grateful to my friend Christa, who took the picture that
long ago.

"I hardly remember baby Keena. And Marja
doesn't remember her at all," Dennis said, staring at
the picture in his hand.

"You both were still so little. And Marit and Liesel weren't born yet," I said. "God took Keena back home, and now she is our guardian angel in heaven."

"I know," Dennis said with a smile. "She's watching over our family. Especially over Marja and Marit, since they are closest to her in age."

Dennis returned the picture, pocketed the money, and said, "Thanks, Mom." He turned away, already focused on how to spend his hard-earned cash. I gently replaced the picture in my wallet and thought about the most painful time of my life.

That cold autumn day, eight years earlier, I had stood, encircled by my family, at the graveside service for my newborn third child. Large pines shadowed the open grave, which looked like a wound in the ground. I glanced at the covered pile of dirt next to it and shivered.

The late fall sun brightened the roses and carnations hiding the tiny pink coffin. I turned my head, certain that the sun would never shine for me again. A haze of trees and people surrounded me, and the wind sighed in the trees as if in sympathy.

My husband, Gary, slipped his hand in mine. Four-year-old Dennis, my firstborn, held on to his grandpa's hand and watched the coffin with a frown. He stood stiff and straight, like a little soldier, but eighteen-month-old Marja wriggled in her grandma's arms, trying to reach the flowers. I fixed my burning eyes on the small coffin with its loved burden. After this day nothing would be left of a child that I had hardly seen, nothing but memories.

The preacher said something about her soul being too perfect for her small body, and I bit my lips. I knew she was in heaven now, waiting for me, but the thought didn't give me any comfort. The service came to an end. I stepped away from the grave, feeling lost and empty. There was nothing there for me anymore.

My friend Christa hugged me. "I've taken pictures," she said.

I swallowed my tears. "I don't want to remember this day."

"I can't imagine how painful this all is for you," she said. "But later, in a few years maybe, you'll be glad for the pictures."

Gary, tall and handsome in his dark blue suit, led us to his father's Chrysler. For a moment I became aware of my dumpy figure. My body hadn't healed yet from giving birth, and not caring what I looked like, I had shrouded myself in a dark blue maternity dress. I felt old and worn out, distanced from Gary, still a good-looking young father, and from our other two children.

"Will you be all right?" Grandma asked before she and Grandpa left. Concern darkened her blue eyes behind the rhinestone glasses.

"Yes. Gary will take care of me."

When they were gone, I lay down on the couch. I felt lost, lonely, heartbroken, and deserted by everyone. Even God. Why had He done this to me? Somehow, I knew that He still loved me, and somehow, I knew that there was a purpose to all this, but I didn't want to think about it.

I picked tiny Marja up as she toddled by, trying to get a measure of comfort from my smallest, herself still a baby. I held her to my aching breasts, but she wouldn't nurse anymore. She wiggled out of my arms and stood on her unsteady legs. With a sigh, I laid back on the sofa, trying to think of nothing.

Gary put the kids to bed that night, in order to give me as much rest as he could. But when he came out of Dennis's room, I forced myself off the couch and went into the children's rooms to have prayers with them.

Little Marja, looking like a small angel, folded her chubby arms across her chest. She repeated the prayer after me, then snuggled into her blanket and smiled. Her happiness made me realize that she didn't understand what had happened earlier.

I went into Dennis's room. He had already said his own prayers, but I asked him to kneel with me on the yellow shag next to his bed. He folded his arms and prayed, "Dear Heavenly Father, bless Mamma and Dad, and Marja, and Grandpa and Grandma."

He stopped, regarded me with big, solemn eyes, and continued, "Bless the new baby, too, so she won't cry in her grave."

A jolt of misery constricted my chest, but I wasn't going to cry in front of Dennis. He was worried enough already.

When he was done with his prayers, I tucked him into bed. His small face was serious.

I kissed his cheek and said, "Your little sister isn't in the grave, sweetheart. What we put into the grave is only her body." He wrinkled his brow.

How could I explain something like this to a four-year-old? Then, I remembered an analogy I'd heard in church. It might help Dennis understand what had happened, so he wouldn't worry.

"The baby's body is like a glove," I explained. "Without your hand in it, a glove is just a piece of clothing. It can't move or do anything, just like the baby's body is now. But when you put your hand into the glove, it can move and do things. Your hand is like the baby's soul, the real baby. The body we buried today is just the glove, without anything to make it wiggle. Our baby is in heaven with God and Jesus."

"Okay." Dennis lay back on his pillow and yawned. "I'm glad she doesn't have to live in the cold earth," he said, and sighed.

Suddenly the truth of what I had tried to explain to my son unfolded for me. As I kissed Dennis and left his room, a warm feeling of comfort and reassurance spread through my aching body. My grief for the baby hadn't diminished, and I still mourned the life she would have brought to my family, but somehow I felt better. God had already given me His comfort, in the form of the two angels he let me keep, Dennis and Marja.

~Sonja Herbert

Uphill Battles and
Bountiful Blessings

I spoke to you when you were born. Be still.
Know I am God. I speak to you through
the trees of the forests. Be still. Know I am
God. I speak to you through the valleys
and the hills. Be still. Know I am God.
I speak to you through the waves of the
sea. Be still. Know I am God. I speak
to you through the dew of the morn-
ing. Be still. Know I am God. I speak
to you through the peace of the eve-
ning. Be still. Know I am God.
I speak to you through the brilliant stars.
Be still. Know I am God. I will speak to
you when you are alone. Be still. Know
I am God. I will speak to you through-
out Eternity. Be still. Know I am God.

—*The Essene Gospel of Peace*

Pace. It seemed that's all I did the hot, humid
month of June when I was twenty years old

and halfway through my college education. Every day, I watched for the letter carrier to come down the block, and the interminable wait dragged on. I tried to keep myself busy—reading, embroidering, sweeping the sidewalk, helping my mom with chores around the house—whatever I could find to do close to home. My summer job kept me busy on weekends, but weekdays afforded me plenty of time to stew. So that's what I did. *Where was it? Where was my acceptance letter?*

In May, I'd graduated from junior college, and all the hustle and bustle of campus life and my various classes came to a sudden halt. For two years, I had worked hard to meet the course requirements of my associate's degree and simultaneously to fulfill the requirements for entrance to a college of the City University of New York. I'd applied myself to my studies and made good grades. I'd prepared well and felt my acceptance to Hunter College a sure thing. So, *where was that delinquent acceptance letter?*

After weeks of greeting our mail carrier with "Anything from Hunter?" and his shaking his head in reply, he finally "delivered" at the end of June. He approached our house with a grin, the coveted letter in hand, and chuckled when I grabbed the envelope and ripped it open right there on the sidewalk.

This was to be a moment of triumph, of

success achieved. My hands shook with excitement as I tore back the flap, but when I read the curt message inside, I was stunned. "We regret to inform you . . ." My mind raced as only a twenty-year-old's can. *What? This cannot be happening. This violates all cosmic rules! What happened to the law of cause and effect?* I had met the requirements and given it my best effort. I should have attained the predicted outcome. Little did I know or appreciate how blessed I'd been that it had always happened that way before. How simple! How logical! How in control I'd always felt! Life had been difficult at times and frequently required great effort, but it had always played fair and followed my same straightforward formula for success.

I had no idea what to do next. Acceptance to Hunter College, back in the 1960s, was like winning a scholarship. No tuition! And that certainly would help make up for the expenses of my freshman and sophomore years. My parents planned to put all four of their daughters through higher education. I couldn't ask them to spend more money for mine now that the free tuition of Hunter was being denied.

With the fall semester only two months away, I had no time to apply elsewhere. If college was no longer possible, could I find a job? I had majored in liberal arts. Except for my limited typing ability, I had no marketable skills. Besides, I was timid, and the "real world" frightened me. I had made no contingency plans. Because I had done well, taken the required courses, achieved the required grades, and was a resident of New York City, didn't Hunter *have* to accept me? After all, I had played by their rules for two years.

I ran into the house, letting the screen door bang behind me, and telephoned the Hunter Admissions Office. "You lack the foreign language credits," they informed me. "But that's impossible," I protested. "I completed two semesters of German and plan to take the third term in my junior year." They would not budge, but maintained that some technicality kept them from accepting my first semester of German.

Next, I telephoned my junior college and questioned the academic dean. He graciously contacted Hunter on my behalf, only to learn that Dean Hollinghurst, the one person who could have provided some guidance, had gone on vacation. Completely frustrated with all the people who might have helped, I turned my thinking toward God. I believed when a person tried their hardest, God blessed their efforts with success. My goal was honorable, and I had the ability to attain it. Was I asking too much? For days, I struggled with God and pored over other college catalogs at the library, searching in vain for a workable solution. I examined my motives, my methods, and myself. What was the magic formula for miracles? I wondered.

No answers, no insight came all week. Frustrated and exhausted, I went to my room after lunch one day, closed the door, and fell to my knees. This was not my customary posture for praying, but I wanted to submit to God's will and this seemed appropriate. With tears in my eyes, and my knees pressing against the hard wooden floor, I prayed, "Dear Lord, I don't know what to do. I don't know if I'm supposed to continue my studies or find a job. I don't know where I can go to school. I don't know where I can go to work. I'm in such a muddle. But the Bible says you have a plan for my life. Help me to be still so I can discover what you want me to do. Lord, I put it all into your hands." At wits' end, my emotions taut, my soul aching with despair, I gave it all up to God.

Later that afternoon, my older sister came home from her teaching job. "How 'bout a swim at Blue Mountain Lake?" she suggested. It was the last day of the school year, and she was ready for the summer fun to begin. I grabbed my suit and off we went. The lake, only forty-five minutes from home, might well have been halfway around the globe, so far did I feel transported from my troubles. The sunshine sparkled across the water. The blue sky played backdrop to an occasional cumulus cloud. I lay on my back on the soft and glistening sand. Motionless, I let the quiet summer breezes blow over me. Time seemed suspended as I stared into the clear sky and thought of nothing at all.

I had relinquished my problem and my future to God, and without any effort of will on my part, the anxiety drifted away with nature's breeze. So complete was my mental and emotional transformation, I forgot I ever had a problem to solve. When we returned home, I felt refreshed and rejuvenated.

Mom was waiting at the front door with some stunning news to share. "Helene." She beamed. "You'll never believe it. Dean Gabbert called. He reached Dr. Hollinghurst this afternoon, and she'll admit you in September. All you have to do is find an approved German class this summer and complete it successfully."

I could not believe my ears. Two years of planning and studying, a month of waiting, and a week of fretting had changed nothing. Then, I relinquished my efforts to the Lord, and all was turned around in an afternoon—an afternoon I had spent lost in the tranquility of God and his creation.

My story doesn't end there. I had to find an approved course and, having found one, plead for admission to a class that was already overenrolled. I had to find transportation to the school because I didn't have a car or a driver's license. And finally, I had to work hard to pass a difficult course. Nineteenth-Century German Literature was no piece of apple strudel (especially without a nineteenth-century German dictionary). My expertise was not, and never will be, nineteenth-century anything, no less a foreign language. I had to look up every word I read, and after each two-hour class and the two-hour roundtrip commute, my homework took me three hours each day and six on weekends.

What a summer I spent! Nevertheless, I knew God had me back on the right path. I completed the six-week course with a B and, in September, began my junior year at Hunter College.

It was a summer of uphill battles, but it taught me a great lesson. Life is not under *my* control. I can apply myself, work hard, set and achieve one goal after the next, but it is God who establishes my steps and bestows his blessings. The same God who created the universe and set the moon and stars in their courses, created me. His greatest desire is for me to turn to him in every circumstance of my life. When I dwell in Him, I receive His blessings.

~Helene C. Kuoni

So, I Pray

I am suffering and in pain.
Rescue me, O God, by your saving power.
Then I will praise God's name with singing,
and I will honor him with thanksgiving.
For this will please the Lord more than
sacrificing cattle, more than presenting a bull
with its horns and hooves.
The humble will see their God at work and be
glad.
Let all who seek God's help be encouraged.
For the Lord hears the cries of the needy;
he does not despise his imprisoned people.

—Psalm 69:29–33

My family was poor when I was a child. My mother worked endlessly to provide for us, but we seldom had enough food or clothing. I day-dreamed of becoming successful and was determined that I wouldn't struggle as my mother had done. I wanted a decent home and enough money to get by. I had no idea of how this would happen, but

I had hopes of perhaps having a career as either an artist or a writer. As the years passed, I realized that my dreams would never come true. It turned out that I would never finish high school or attend a college.

I married just after I turned eighteen and had my first child by the time I was nineteen. I was blessed with four more children, but my marriage was very unstable and ended in divorce. I was left alone with the children as my ex-husband moved on. I didn't pray much, except to silently argue with God and ask Him why my life had been such a struggle. I surely wasn't living the dream I had wanted.

My life was a constant battle to put food on the table and care for my children. We lived in state after state, barely getting by except for the kindness of friends and family. My hopes of ever having anything were gone. Maybe I had set my standards too high. I had plans of marrying again, but my fiancée passed away suddenly at the age of forty. My mother followed only three years later. I felt so lost. How could God do this to me? Hadn't I suffered enough?

We lived in many large cities, but the crime and confusion finally got the best of me. I feared for my family's safety. After several years, we moved to a small town in Tennessee. My children grew, married, and left home. I had beautiful grandchildren and was able to see them often, since most of them lived close by, but sometimes I felt so alone. Something was missing in my life.

I prayed and asked God why I even existed. What was my purpose—to live in this world just to struggle every day to get by? I was an adult, capable of making rational decisions. Why did everything I attempt fail so miserably? I began to think that God didn't care. I would find out many years later how wrong I had been.

Eventually, I found a job that paid better than most of the jobs in the small town in which I now lived. I began working for a drywall company and jokingly told several new homeowners that I only worked on new houses and would never be fortunate enough to live in one. Though my job didn't make me rich, at least it made it possible to survive. I found an rundown old house for sale and took out a small loan at the bank. I'd never be able to afford the repairs, but for the time being, it was a roof over my head.

Still, I felt that my life was going downhill. At twenty-five, one of my daughters had become addicted to drugs. I prayed that God would keep her safe. She knew she had a terrible problem and willingly gave me custody of her two children, a three-year-old girl with mild cerebral palsy, and a six-year-old boy with ADHD. I stared down at my hands and prayed silently in front of the juvenile officer before I signed the papers that would give me legal custody. "God, what will I do now?" I thought.

I was fifty-one, facing bankruptcy, my health was slowly declining, and I lived in an old shack. The house was large enough for us, but the foundation was slipping, and the roof leaked. I could never take two small children to live in that mess, but I had no other choice. At bedtime, the three of us would all curl up in the living room, the only room that didn't leak. I slept in a recliner, the boy on the couch, and the girl on a small cot.

After the kids and I spent three more years of hot summers with only a tiny air conditioner, and freezing winters using a kerosene heater, my son-in-law noticed an announcement in the local paper. The Community Development Center had given our county a grant, and they were taking applications for new housing. Although I was certain I would fit the requirements, I doubted that, with the way my luck was running, I would get any further than filling out the application.

I begged God to let us be approved for a new home. One day, I called a dear friend, who happened to be a pastor, with the news that I was applying for a grant to have a new house built. I asked him to pray for us. He told me that he would, and then he said words that I would never forget. "If God wants you to have it, you will have it."

All this time, I had been asking God for specific things. I had never turned anything over to Him before. I had always tried to fix situations on my own. Now, I learned to pray a different way. "Dear God, if this is in your plan for me, please let it be." God knew what I needed, and he never gave me more than I could bear. I put everything in God's hands.

Several months later, I received a phone call from a representative of the organization that headed the housing project. "You are right at the top of the list," the woman exclaimed. I couldn't believe what I was hearing. Out of thirty-six applications, I was at the top! The waiting had been almost unbearable, and it would be several more months before I would know the final decision. Even so, I had a good feeling about it, although I wasn't sure why.

Our home was built in October 2004. Members of a local community service brought us beds and appliances. My prayers had been answered, and all I had done was turn it over to God. My daughter is now free of the drugs that once controlled her and is trying desperately to make a life for herself and, eventually, her children.

Because of God, I have been able to help my family. I was there when they needed me, and that's what really counted. Eventually, I was able to find wonderful specialists for the children. The little girl is walking more without the use of her walker, and the boy has his ADHD under control.

As for my writing, it's only part time at the moment, because I now know that my purpose in life is whatever God has planned for me. With his help, I know it will turn out perfectly. I no longer question why I am here, and I no longer feel alone. God is only a prayer away. No matter what may come, I know God and I can handle it. He is always welcome in the home He gave us.

~Connie R. Smith

Big Dreams in a Small Boat

Dear God, be good to me, the sea is
so wide, and my boat is so small.

—*Breton Fisherman's Prayer*

There comes a time in every single mother's life when you wonder if you really can do a good job raising your kids alone. For me, that time comes every September, when school starts. This year proved no different.

My son Mikey was now fourteen—and a freshman. For him, life at a small-town all-American high school would be as stereotypical as it gets: more guy pals to hang with, more homework to do, and more girls calling every night. And, most important, more football.

Football. Sure, I knew what football was—more or less. I'd been raised by a man obsessed with the sport, in a home where the TV was always tuned to ESPN; I'd gone to Purdue, a Big Ten school where football was practically a religion; and I lived in Massachusetts, where rooting for the New England

Patriots is obligatory. I'd even had my own brush with greatness, having once sat next to Doug Flutie on a plane. Okay, so I didn't recognize him, but even I'd heard about that Hail Mary pass at Boston College.

Hail Marys aside, football was a father/son thing. True, I'd filled in as a substitute dad on other occasions in the past. I cheered Mikey on at all his soccer games, taught him to paddle a canoe, helped him build a car for the Pinewood Derby. I'd done all a mom could do—and then some. But I was no Doug Flutie.

The freshman football team began practice in late summer before school even began. I wrote the $180 check to cover the price of Mikey's new gear. I took him to the sporting goods store to buy cleats. I signed up to sell hot dogs at the snack bar during the games. I washed his uniforms and drove him back and forth across town to practice and cooked huge meals to feed the ever-rumbling stomach that fuels the freshman football player. And I cried.

"What's the matter, Mom?" Mikey asked me on our way home from yet another practice.

"It's nothing," I said, smoothing away the tear that ran down my cheek.

"Are you *crying?*" The fourteen-year-old looked at me the way his fully grown counterparts looked at us women sometimes, as if we were from another planet.

"Maybe." I sniffed.

"Why?"

I could tell by his voice he wasn't sure he wanted to know. "I just feel bad for you sometimes." I ruffled the curls on his head. "You know, stuck with me all the time."

"Hands on the wheel, Mom."

"Right." I withdrew my hand.

"I don't mind." Mikey said by way of apology. "Being stuck with you, I mean."

"But I see all those other dads there with their sons."

Mikey considered this. "Mom, there are always more moms than dads there."

I stared at him. "You're right. You're absolutely right." I smiled. The boy who never did his math homework could count, after all. "Still, you must wish your dad could come to a game."

Mikey didn't say anything. His father lived across the country in California. Mikey visited him there several times a year, but his father had never been to Massachusetts to see him. Never seen his room or met his friends or been to his school.

I was ashamed to say that even though that was his father's choice, it was a choice that secretly pleased me very much. I made a mental note to ask God for forgiveness on that one.

"Mikey," I said gently, "if you want, you could invite him to a game. Or if you're uncomfortable doing that, I could invite him for you."

Mikey turned his head away. "I'll think about it."

I didn't say anything. I knew that he'd rather not invite his dad, than invite him and have him not come. The disappointment would be too great. He was stuck with me, whether he liked it or not. Whether I was up to the task or not.

Since that day I've said the Breton Fisherman's Prayer for me and my son Mikey every night. Because the hardest part of being a single mom is this: Your boat is so small, and your hopes and dreams for your child are so big. *Dear God, be good to us.*

~Paula Munier

Family Portrait

*As the deer longs for streams of water, so
I long for you, O God. I thirst for God, the
living God. When can I go and stand before
him? Day and night I have only tears for
food, while my enemies continually taunt me,
saying, "Where is this God of yours?" My
heart is breaking as I remember how it used
to be: I walked among the crowds of worship-
ers, leading a great procession to the house of
God, singing for joy and giving thanks amid
the sound of a great celebration! Why am
I discouraged? Why is my heart so sad?
I will put my hope in God! I will praise
him again—my Savior and my God!*

—Psalm 42:1–6

The year 1996 began as one of the best years of my life. Married twenty-eight years, Johnnie and I were more in love than ever. We'd raised two beautiful daughters, Karyn and Melinda, and were about to adopt a son, eight-year-old Robert.

I was on the Praise Team at our church, and we were always willing to serve where needed, but foster parenting was our full-time ministry, a way to show God's love to troubled children. In sixteen years, we had kept more than 100 children, and after two years of constant love and reassurance, our last child, seventeen-year-old Kelly, was finally beginning to trust. Ours was a home full of love, laughter, and faith.

When we learned in March that Melinda and her husband, Matt, were expecting a baby, our joy was complete, our family portrait perfect, everything just as it should be. I felt so blessed, but I never took it for granted. I knew my happiness was a gift from God and I thanked Him for it every day. I never dreamed that our home would soon be empty, our hearts broken, and our lives turned upside down.

At forty-six, Johnnie was handsome and fit, all construction-hardened muscle, the rock I had leaned on since I was fourteen. When an EKG in late March found four blockages in his heart, we were stunned. After quadruple bypass surgery, he left the hospital trembling and hesitant. He was often weepy and wouldn't let me out of his sight. The doctor warned that serious clinical depression and anxiety were possible after heart surgery, but the change was profound and frightened all of us. I struggled to reassure the children and keep things as normal as possible.

Melinda and Matt hoped to encourage him with the first tape-recording of their baby's heartbeat a couple of weeks later. But the doctor couldn't find one. Our baby, so loved, so wanted, had died.

It seemed that before we could stop reeling from one catastrophe, another blindsided us. During the next few weeks, Melinda and our niece Cristy were each in a terrible auto accident, both cars totaled. Thankfully, both walked away uninjured. But then, on June 11, another car crash—Karyn, only twenty-five, was unconscious and not expected to live.

Minute by minute, the days passed as Karyn hung on in a deep coma, always one heartbeat from death. Johnnie and I camped outside intensive care around the clock. Robert's adoption had begun, so he was with relatives, but our Kelly was ripped from us by Children Services and placed in another foster home. In her grief and terror, she screamed that she hated us, that we were just like everyone else in her life, that she couldn't trust anyone. All I could answer was, "I know, baby. I'm sorry. I love you." Within days, she had run away.

For weeks, our home sat abandoned. Still in a coma, Karyn finally came off life support and was moved to a rehab hospital. Every morning, attendants put straps around her head and chest to hold her upright in a wheelchair. Under empty eyes, a shimmering line of drool ran from her slack lip to her knee. As her injured brain contorted her body into a frightening caricature of our lovely Karyn, I talked and sang to her, prayed for her, and begged her to come back to us.

Johnnie, my partner, my love, was gone, replaced by a near stranger. Antidepressants were no help; he had emotionally shut down. I needed so badly for him to hold me, pray with me, and tell me everything would be okay, but he seemed detached from everyone and everything. When, after two months, doctors said there was no hope left that Karyn would wake up, he barely noticed.

Weeks later, their report changed again. They said Karyn might emerge from the coma but be unable to move, speak, see, or hear. If she woke up, we might not even know it.

Only a few months before, I was positive that the worst thing this life could bring me was the death of my child. Now, with my faith gone, I knew better. Right or wrong, my constant prayer was that my daughter would die.

Finally the strain of denial became too much for Johnnie; he collapsed and was hospitalized. I raced between two hospitals, stretched so thin I thought

I would come apart. Then, within days, Melinda lost another baby, a little girl.

I began to see myself as I imagined others saw me. How could anyone bear to be near me—a barren and forsaken woman huddled under a dark cloud of misery, her life being slowly sucked away one loved one at a time? I wanted so badly to run away, to be someone else—a whole person who laughed, bought shoes, and worried if her pants were too tight. But there was no escape for me anywhere. My life was hospitals, grieving children, and empty arms.

I put up a good front, going through the motions. I still prayed, but now my soul was a dry, dead thing, and I simply prayed for mercy. I sought comfort in music, but nothing satisfied me—they were just empty words. An old gospel song came to mind, but I couldn't quite remember it, and I asked around, but nobody had it. Then one day, in a checkout line, I idly looked through a bin of bargain cassettes, and suddenly there it was! I bought it, hurried to my car, and shoved it into the tape player. As the cherished old hymns filled the car, fresh tears choked me. Karyn would never hear music again. After ministering to children all my life, I would never rock grandchildren or sing them to sleep. Overwhelmed by grief and loss, I almost didn't hear the sweet, familiar song, "Somebody's Praying." The words reached out to me, and into me, and I thought I felt the gentle rain of hope on my parched soul. Could it be that as our family stumbled through this dark wilderness, someone had been praying for us? That God's people weren't afraid to be near us, but their strong arms were bearing us up, crying out to the Master to rescue us? Was our God, even now, grieving with us and longing to comfort us? And the answer came to me there, in the stillness of my parked car, as the peace of God swelled within me, and my soul began to sing again. Our God had not turned His back on us. He would bring us through this into His light, if we would simply trust Him.

Our family portrait is a little different today, but we're still blessed beyond anything we deserve. We've been through a lot, and I'm sure it shows. But Karyn is here, wide-awake, happy, and living proof that medical science has nothing on the Great Physician. Her life, like ours, is not quite what she planned, but it's a good life, full of praise and purpose. As for Melinda and Matt, after two miscarriages and two years of infertility, God has given them two healthy children, Avery and Matthew.

Nearly two years after she left us, Kelly came home and, with God's help, has forgiven us. She and her husband, another wonderful Matt, have given us two more healthy, precious grandchildren—Payton and Presley. Robert is almost a man now, strong and loving, just like his Dad. And Johnnie, my love, my rock, is here, too. We are restored.

We've known unbearable pain and unspeakable joy, and, with God's help, we have borne them both. I know people wonder, sometimes, why God allowed us to be swept down a path we would have never willingly taken, to a place full of darkness and suffering.

I don't know. But that dark path led us, ultimately, to where we are now. It's not the peaceful "perfect" place we left in March 1996, but another place full of love, faith, and family. A place where we are all stronger and where, despite everything that has happened, we are still blessed and held safely in His arms. And now we know for sure what we once only believed. No matter where life takes us, our God is faithful.

~*Linda Darby Hughes*

Roots and Wings

*Heavenly Father, bless our children with
healthful bodies, with good understandings,
with the graces and gifts of your Spirit,
with sweet dispositions and holy habits.*

—Jeremy Taylor

My daughter, husband, and I are on our way to take our son Chase to college for the first time. The pickup truck, loaded with nine months' worth of living necessities, is quiet. Each of us is alone with our thoughts. We know that nothing will ever be the same again, but we aren't ready to accept it. Of course, we'll still be a family, but we won't be together on a daily basis anymore.

And, just as I did on Chase's first day of kindergarten, I relinquish myself to the fact that I will be turning my son loose, entrusting him to total strangers. The stark reality hits me today as it did back then—I cannot go with him.

I glance at my husband and wonder what he's thinking. It wouldn't surprise me if he, too, was trying to grasp the brevity of time. Wasn't it just yesterday that we brought Chase home from the hospital as a newborn baby, his dark eyes alert and bright, longing even then to take in the whole world? The doctors had told me I might never conceive, but two years after our miracle son was born, we were blessed by a second miracle, the birth of his sister, Chelsea.

My daughter is staring outside, headset on and music blaring. Through her reflection in the window, I see a somewhat lost and sad look on her face, and I swallow hard. Memories of my older sister, Sue, the first of my four siblings to leave the nest, come flooding back. I remember crying myself to sleep her last night at home, knowing that, from that time on, she would become a "guest" in our house. I was angry about the coming changes; changes that I knew were unstoppable.

Chelsea had been displaying similar signs of anger. Just the other day, I overheard her blurt out to her brother, "You promised to go sledding with me for two years and you never did."

Chase shook his head, trying to make sense of her sudden outburst. After all, this was August in Ohio, and the heat and humidity were smothering. Who could think about snow?

He tried to comfort her. "I'll be home often, Chels, even in the winter. I won't be that far away." And he was right; the university he would be attending was only an hour-and-a-half drive.

"Yeah, but when you do come home, you'll want to hang out with your friends," she reminded him.

Chase said nothing. He probably realized she was right.

Finally, I turn my thoughts to my son. After a whirlwind senior year and a summer that disappeared just as quickly, it's down to this moment. But, in all honesty, from the day we found out that I was pregnant with him, these past eighteen years have been a joyful blur of learning, lessons, and love. The baby who started life at only twenty-one inches long is now six-foot-four. He doesn't fit very well in the backseat of our pickup truck, so I let him sit up front by his dad, who happens to be just as tall.

Chase's head is laid back on the headrest, and I can see in the side mirror that his eyes are shut. Gone is the excitement of the summer and talk of how he "can't wait to be out on his own." He, too, has been unusually grouchy these past few days, especially while packing. Maybe the prospect of life on his own has suddenly overwhelmed him.

Then, I realize that I share my children's anger. I thought I would be prepared for this, and materialistically, I was. He had everything he needed for his dorm room and then some. What I hadn't prepared for, though, were the grieflike symptoms that were threatening to overtake me. A division was taking place in my family that I wanted to stop but couldn't.

When my children were born, I had mistakenly assumed that when the time came for them to leave the nest, I would be ready and even willing to watch them fly away. Instead, along with fighting back tears, I found myself wanting to scream at the top of my lungs, "Wait! I'm not ready for this. I need more time."

I want more time to instill in him all the values that I'm certain I forgot to teach him. More time to enlighten him in how to discern true friends from those who just want to use him. More time to instruct him about budgeting his time and money, finding the perfect mate and eating right—the list is endless.

Before I know it, it's time to unload the truck. I still don't have a clue as to what I'm going to say to Chase before we leave. Always full of motherly advice whether my kids want it or not, I, for once, am speechless. Yet, suddenly, it is overwhelmingly important to me to leave him with some words of wisdom—but what?

Finally the last box is shoved into Chase's room. He insists on getting settled after we leave, and I realize that our goodbyes can be put off no longer. I stare at my children as they hug each other with fierce, unashamed affection, and my heart almost breaks when I hear them say they love each other. *Are these the same two kids who used to fight over who could turn the page when we would read to them at bedtime?*

Next comes a bear hug for his dad, and that is exactly what they remind me of: two huge bears seized in an embrace that must last through a time of hibernation. Theirs is a father-and-son bond that will never break but must begin to bend as each needs to learn how to let go.

Then, all too soon, it's my turn. I hear my husband say that there are other parents waiting for our parking spot, and we have to move our truck. I am startled by the hint of fear amidst the sadness and excitement on Chase's face. And that's when I realize; I had been so consumed by my own fear for Chase that it hadn't dawned on me that he would probably experience his own surge of emotions as we drove down the road. Sure, we've had lots of talks in the past year in an attempt to prepare him. But at the time, when this day was in the distant future, it was exciting to think about the prospect of meeting total strangers, strangers with whom he would forge friendships that would last a lifetime. Now that the actual moment of separation was here, I knew I couldn't leave him without something solid to hold on to, something to ease the fear.

I quickly deliver a silent, desperate plea to God, asking for words of comfort. Then, standing on tip-toes, I wrap my arms around this giant of a man who will always be my little boy, and I hear myself say, "Son, don't forget about God. He never forgets about you."

Our watery eyes lock and hold in a moment I will never forget. Somehow I knew these were just the words he needed to hear, yet, I had no idea I was going to say them. And then it dawns on me. The words God just gave to me to minister to Chase had comforted me, as well. God never forgets about any one of us. He sees the transition my husband is going through and says, "Trust Me." He sees the loneliness my daughter is experiencing and says, "Talk to Me." He knows the worry I have over Chase's decision making and reminds me, "I'll pick Chase up when he falls." He sees Chase's own fear of the unknown and says, "Put your hand in Mine."

It took only a few words and a few minutes for God to take the pressure I had mistakenly placed upon myself and to transfer it to where it belonged—in His hands. The Lord gently reminded me that Chase was never truly mine in the first place. I was just the vessel He chose to use to bring Chase into this world, to set into motion the plans He already had for his life. And this is as it should be—this letting go, this spreading of wings. While my influence will be less, my role still needs to be one that will continue to point Chase to that Higher Power.

For the rest of my life, the best advice I can give my children will not be "Don't forget to eat right" or "Choose your friends wisely." The best thing I can do for my children, besides continuing to pray for them, is to continue reminding them that they belong to God. To remind them to place their faith in His promises, especially Hebrews 13:5, "Never will I leave you; never will I forsake you" (NIV). God never forgets about any one of us, even when we forget about Him.

~Connie Sturm Cameron

When It Hurts Too Much to Trust God

I love you, Lord;
you are my strength.
The Lord is my rock, my fortress, and my savior;
my God is my rock, in whom I find protection.
He is my shield, the power that saves me,
and my place of safety.
I called on the Lord, who is worthy of praise,
and he saved me from my enemies.

—Psalm 18:1–3

Covered with mud, I unwound my stiff, aching joints and stood. My water garden was finished. I watched as twelve small goldfish curiously inspected every inch of their new home. My gaze rested for a moment on the frail-looking, nearly beheaded water lily as it lay in its pot in the center of my pond. I looked away quickly because I didn't care if it lived or died. I scooped up the wooden tag that had been in the pot and took it to our basement. Holding it in my shaking hands, I once again read its description: Maroon Sirius Lily. So much for answered prayer, I thought.

I despised that lily because its presence in my pond told my numb and confused brain that God didn't love me at all. While I believed that God loved the whole-wide world, I was convinced that his love didn't extend to me. I tossed the tag in the trash.

You see, my father, whom I hadn't seen since I was a child, had come back into my life. The disheveled and unshaven man who stared back at me when I opened the door to his knock said simply, "I am your father." All I could do was murmur a quiet, "Oh, Lord please help me. . . ." At that moment, I desperately needed assurance of God's love, but He seemed so far away.

Invited in, my father proceeded to tell my husband, Ted, and me that people were trying to poison him, and God had told him he should find me, because I would be able to help him. Later that evening, as we watched him walk, all hunched over, back down the stairs to the street, it was obvious that my father was seriously mentally ill. When a psychiatrist subsequently diagnosed Dad as an incurable paranoid schizophrenic, I felt like a ton of bricks had fallen on me. Recently married and living in our new home, my plans for "living happily ever after" seemed to be gone forever.

Ted and I talked and prayed about what to do. Dad had deserted our family in the midst of the Depression, leaving my mother to raise my sister and me in poverty. I didn't believe that I owed my father anything. Ted, my rock and committed Christian husband, offered, "There's no one else to help your dad since all of his family has given up on him. Let's see what we can do for him and just trust the future to the Lord." Scared and fearful of how our lives might be changed, I reluctantly agreed.

Agonizing days followed as we had him committed to the Spencer State Mental Hospital. On a trial visit back to see his mother, he tried to kill her. The deputy sheriff had driven him back to the hospital, and his mother moved in with one of her other children, where she would be protected from her son. Desperately, I sought the Lord in prayer. "Oh, dear God," I prayed, "please either heal my father or deliver me from this burden that has me so weighted down."

I needed to feel God's presence in my life so badly. Yet, never before in all of my life had I felt that the gates of heaven were closed to my prayers. However, I didn't stop praying. My mind was filled with prayers constantly as I hoped for a sign from God that he was hearing me. In my dulled state of mind, though, I neither saw nor heard an answer.

During the next couple of years, my father was released for more trial periods, but each release was quickly followed by another commitment, as he invariably became a danger to himself and others. When I became angry with God for letting this happen to me, bitterness entered my torn-to-pieces heart. Ted, sensing my utter misery, encouraged me to find a project to occupy my mind and my body. That's when I thought of a garden pool, complete with goldfish and a lily. As I planned my pool, another prayer went up to my Father in heaven. "I'm asking for just one thing, Lord. A water lily for my pond. A bright yellow one, please?" Then I added, disrespectfully, "That is all, Lord. I want a yellow water lily for my fishpond. Surely, you can arrange that, can't you?"

So, I got out my shovel and dug a garden pool to take my mind off my circumstances. Once my pond was ready, I went looking for fish and a yellow water lily. There were several pet shops in town, but only one had a water lily for sale—Maynard's Pet Shop in downtown Charleston. I purchased twelve goldfish from Mr. Maynard at that time, and asked about the color of his one water lily. "Oh, it's maroon," he tossed off casually. I was stunned, for if I had a least favorite color at that time, it was maroon!

Sick at heart, I followed Mr. Maynard to the tank and gazed down at the one lonely lily. Tears filled my eyes, because in addition to the ugly brownish color of its one leaf, this forlorn water plant had suffered an accident, and its head lay over to one side. Offering it to me for 50 cents, Mr. Maynard told me that this one would have sold for $15.00 had it been in good shape. "But lilies are hard to kill," he said, as he promised me my money back if it did not live. Since it was the only lily in town, I accepted it.

If I felt bereft of God's love before, now I was feeling totally rejected by my Lord. Deeply grieved that my prayer had not been answered, I cried all the way home. Childish? Yes! But at that time, I was deeply depressed and I thought and acted like a child. It would be several months before I would put away childish things.

Once the lily was in its pot on the bottom of my pool, I gave it no care at all. If it was to survive, it would have to do so on its own. A mild spring passed into a glorious summer. My garden pool was visible from our bedroom window, and each morning, as soon as my feet hit the floor, I checked on that hated water lily from our bedroom window. And each morning, I was reminded once more of God's lack of care for me. But despite what I thought of that lily and my neglect, its one spindly leaf found its way toward the surface of the pond. I had to admit that it was trying hard to live.

Then something odd began to happen. Maternal instincts, previously unknown to me, began to surface. After all, I realized it wasn't the lily's fault it was the wrong color. So, timidly, I added a little fertilizer to the pot to help it grow, and brand-new, brownish leaves sprouted everywhere. After that, I set about in earnest to make sure it had the proper environment in which to live. As I tended to its needs, my once despised lily became welcome in my pond—even though it was maroon. With every new leaf, my fear of the future subsided even more. One day, it dawned on me that my hatred for the lily had morphed into love in spite of its color.

An inner peace grew within my soul, the numbness I had felt was replaced with a fresh warm feeling—that God was God, and He would be God forever. I surely could trust Him to take care of me—whatever the future held.

One day, a bud appeared beneath a lily pad. First thing each morning, I would stand on our bed and look out our bedroom window, checking on its progress. A short time later, I drew back our drapes and waited a moment for my eyes to adjust to the morning sun. Then, the majesty of God's grace hit me full force. I gazed at the miracle below and realized that God had planned a very special blessing for me—and I had nearly blown it. I had almost let that lily die from neglect, not knowing about God's mysterious ways. I jumped up and down on the bed and screamed for Ted to wake up and look at my lily.

He and I stood there, hugging each other and crying. For, in my fishpond below, the most gorgeous yellow bloom greeted me. God was on His throne and all was right with the world.

My husband and I continued to pray that God would touch my father's heart and turn his life around, and with the advent of medications for the mentally ill, we finally saw a miraculous answer to our prayers. When his mind cleared and his emotions stabilized, my father came to know God and became a changed man. The promise of Psalm 27:13 was mine. I saw the "goodness of the Lord in the land of the living."

~Evelyn Rhodes Smith

Everything by Design

Good and gracious God, on this holy night
you gave us your son. The Lord of the
universe, wrapped in swaddling clothes,
the Savior of all, lying in a manger. On
this holy night draw us into the mystery of
your love. Join our voices with the heavenly
host, that we may sing your glory on high.
Give us a place among the shepherds, that
we may find the one for whom we have
waited. Jesus Christ, your Word made
flesh, who lives and reigns with you in the
unity of the Holy Spirit in the splendor
of eternal light. God forever and ever.

—Prayer for Chritmas Eve

We were not professional singers. We were only a small percentage of a large congregation, filled with the desire to sing for God and share His love with those who were seeking a deeper relationship with Him. Our medium was a Christmas cantata.

Practices began in early September. Every Sunday night we gathered to learn songs and correct intonation problems. We worked hard to enunciate and phrase the lyrics of the songs unanimously in an effort to sound like a choir.

As December approached, we still had several songs to learn, but the busyness of the season kept many members, including myself, away from our rehearsals. The intonation problems continued, and the sopranos were flat while the tenors were sharp. The altos were not loud enough, and the solo parts had yet to be assigned. One evening after practice, I brought my worries to the choir director, who happened to be a personal friend of mine.

After listening to my concerns, she collapsed in her chair and burst into tears. She had her own set of problems: too much to do and not enough hands to do it. The pressure was mounting, and the situation with the choir was the straw that broke the camel's back. Frustration had won the moment.

I was determined not to let these feelings of defeat prevail. I came away from our discussion with a renewed fervor to pray our project through to a successful completion. I solicited the help of other prayer warriors in the congregation, and night after night, we fasted and prayed for the cantata and the problems we were experiencing. The Sunday following my discussion with our choir director, the choir began to pray as a team before and after each rehearsal.

My prayer focus was the members of the choir. I wanted us all to forget the commercialism and the busyness of a contemporary Christmas and concentrate on the birth of our Savior. I prayed that God would fill our hearts with awe as we recognized the precious gift given to the world on that sacred night so many years ago. Little did I know, the prayer for the choir would be answered one heart at a time, starting with mine.

One evening, as the narrator rehearsed the lines to be spoken between the songs, she said something my ears had heard every Christmas for forty years—but for some reason, this time my *heart* heard it, too.

"Jesus was born in a stable—the place where sacrificial animals were born," she said. "Mary didn't just give birth to a son; she gave birth to a Lamb. And this Lamb would take away the sin of mankind through the shedding of His blood in the ultimate sacrifice. A common manger became His throne. A lowly stable became His palace, and a tiny, obscure town became the place where the most important person the world has ever known was born."

Suddenly it hit me. The Word became flesh to fulfill God's plan of redemption. By *design*, there was no room for Mary and Joseph in the inn. By *design*,

Jesus was born in a stable. By *design*, wealthy kings and poor shepherds would bow down and worship Him and bring Him gifts. A miracle occurred in an ordinary stable in an ordinary town, and the world would never be the same again.

In a fleeting second, I felt my heart of ice begin to melt. That night, I was filled with what I imagined was the same awe and wonder that the shepherds and wise men experienced when they first met Jesus. I knew the adult Jesus well—the humble man who healed the sick, raised the dead, and died on a cross, but I had never experienced baby Jesus. I had never given any real thought to the profound sequence of events surrounding His birth.

For several days, I basked in the warmth of the revelation I'd received. Eventually, I shared my feelings with several members of the choir, who admitted they had experienced something similar, even though other parts of the cantata touched their hearts in different ways.

Over the next few weeks, I watched my fellow choir members became more devoted and humble, and I realized we were beginning to understand the real reason for our singing. Suddenly, the importance of the message we had been ordained to convey through a Christmas musical intensified. We were ordinary people, but the shepherds had been ordinary people, too, and they were chosen to convey the same joyful news. Our method may have been different, but the essence of the 2,000-year-old message remained unchanged.

A last appeal to the congregation for volunteers yielded a great harvest. Many people came forward to assist with costumes, publicity, scenery, and lighting. All choir members made Sunday-night rehearsals a priority, and as a result, intonation problems began to disappear. The issues we faced earlier began to resolve themselves. Solos were assigned, and the soloists worked hard to learn their parts quickly. Frustration was replaced with joy, a deepening love for one another, and a tremendous sense of peace. In the midst of our prayer time one night, the Lord reminded me that the prayers of the righteous are powerful and effective. We were seeing God's hand at work through the power of prayer.

Excitement grew as opening night drew closer, and when it arrived, we sang our hearts out. The feelings we had experienced weeks earlier gave birth to songs full of emotion. And when it was over, just a few days before Christmas, we ended our cantata with prayer. We expressed gratitude for the struggles we had encountered that led us to call upon God for His help. By doing so, God moved us from a place of complacency to a place of humility.

Like the wise men, we recognized that the gifts we brought to give to Jesus—the gifts of our voices and subsequently ourselves—paled in comparison to what God the Father first gave to us. We all were changed and we knew it. Christmas had taken on a new, more sacred meaning, and we dared not look back lest we lose sight of the One who is coming again, not as a helpless baby, but as the King of kings and Lord of lords.

~Elisa Yager

Neither Alone
Nor Forsaken

I hear no voice, I feel no touch,
I see no glory bright;
But yet I know that God is near,
In darkness as in light.

He watches ever by my side,
And hears my whispered prayer:
The Father for His little child
Both night and day doth care.

—Child's Evening Hymn

BOOM! Thunder shook us children awake. CRACK! My younger brother called out. Soon Mom was at his bedside, comforting him. CRASH! I leaped from my bed and joined my family in my brother's room.

My brother stayed in bed, and Mom and I lay on the floor as she told us stories about the thunder and lightning. "God's angels are bowling," she said. An especially loud clap was "the angels getting a strike."

Bright lightning was heaven's scoreboard, celebrating the winner. We forgot our fear, as with each passing peal we guessed how many pins the angels had hit. Before the angels threw gutter balls, we had gone back to bed, ready to sleep, secure in Mom's and God's love.

God's love anchored itself in me as I attended church, Sunday school, and youth group. My faith grew as I moved through childhood and young adulthood. God's constant, provident presence was expressed in a Swedish hymn my teachers taught us: "Children of the Heavenly Father." The verses memorized decades ago still speak to me, and the precious words taught me that God is with me, even when I am not necessarily with God.

Throughout the Bible, God chose individuals and tribes and promised to be with them always, no matter what. Noah, Abraham, Joseph, Moses, Joshua, David, the prophets, and the disciples all had God walking with them and leading them. Their trials were typhoons compared to my little squalls. Their examples inspired and humbled me. They taught me that God is faithful and trustworthy.

As I matured, regular prayer time taught me more about being God's child. How I prayed varied, but sometimes, I sat quietly and consciously in God's presence. Sometimes, I included hymns, meditating on a Bible verse, or journaling. Often, it was like a conversation. Those conversational prayers or short remarks to the Almighty occurred throughout the day. All methods of prayer reminded me that God desires a relationship with me, that God loves me more than I can imagine, and that God is ultimately in charge.

One Sunday morning, many years later, a loved one lay near death in a hospital ward that allowed no visitors, including me. From the time I recognized the illness, I begged God for my loved one's healing and restoration. For myself, I asked for wisdom and guidance. Having no family close by, I felt terribly alone. During the darkest time, my emotions strangled my ability to talk, in person or on the phone. I was physically unable to speak to friends and unwilling to burden them with my heartbreak. They had done their best to listen to me and comfort me through this tempest. Their prayers gave me some comfort, but I had to make decisions that were solely mine.

That morning, even my clergy were unavailable. All I could do was pray with silent desperation. Part pleading, part self-pity, I poured out my frantic fears. Caregivers surrounded my loved one, but I was alone. What should I do? I wondered. Find a nursing home for my loved one? Plan a funeral?

I gulped, trying to muster courage and voice to call the hospital ward for information on my loved one's condition. I stood by the phone, wringing my hands, my mind a jumble of feelings. Forcing myself to take deep, slow breaths did not calm me. I still could not pick up the phone. Then, as if lightning hit, my thoughts cleared and, in my mind, I saw Jesus on the cross. God watched His own son die. I raised my clenched hands to heaven and sobbed, "You know! You know!" God knew the agony of enduring a loved one's painful, humiliating death. I was not alone, after all. The Creator of the universe was with me and with my loved one. God had not forsaken me.

I remembered Jesus, preparing His disciples for His death and resurrection, saying to them, "No, I will not abandon you as orphans—I will come to you" (John 14:18). I knew that Jesus would keep His word and console and come for both my loved one and me. How He would do that was up to Him. The same God who brought the Israelites safely across the Red Sea would see us through this crisis. I had to trust.

That storm has passed. Jesus kept His promise and called my loved one out of this life. He came to me by providing everything I needed when I needed it. Very often, this provision came in the form of other people who checked on me daily. They took me out, prayed for me, shared jokes, expressed concern, and simply listened. Compassionate clergy prayed with, and for, my loved one and me throughout the ordeal. They helped me seek proper care and intervention for him, and walked with us through the storm. A loving church family let me cry week after week at services, offering hugs and withholding judgment. Skilled and caring medical, financial, and legal professionals worked to make a bad situation better. God also gave me meaningful work, a life-saver I clung to amid the wreckage.

A black cloud hung over me during those years. As time went on and my grief lifted, I told a friend I felt as if I had been hiding under the covers for a long time, and now it was safe to peek out into the light. Going through this experience has made the dark days less dark and the bright days brighter. I praise God many times a day for the good things I have been given and the lessons I have learned. I have a new perspective about what's really important and can usually laugh about things that would have angered me before. If things are out of order, if I'm running five minutes late, if plans go awry, what difference does it make in life's larger picture? Loving others, showing them compassion and respect, and spending time with God are much more important.

Life is full of dazzling moments, ordinary times, and periods of utter darkness. Though my life is peaceful now, I am not exempt from future storms. Ultimately, what matters is acknowledging God's presence and trusting him in every moment of my life.

As a child waiting for the thunder and lightning to fade, I had no idea the stormy life seas on which I would sail. What I learned as a child is still true. We may not sense a physical presence, but God is ever near, loving His children through darkness and light, storm and calm.

~*Jane Heitman*

Lessons from the Lord

Oh, how my soul praises the Lord.
How my spirit rejoices in God my Savior!
For he took notice of his lowly servant girl,
    and from now on all generations will call
    me blessed.
For the Mighty One is holy,
    and he has done great things for me.
He shows mercy from generation to generation
    to all who fear him.
His mighty arm has done tremendous things!
    He has scattered the proud and haughty ones.
He has brought down princes from their thrones and
    exalted the humble.
He has filled the hungry with good things
    and sent the rich away with empty hands.
He has helped his servant Israel
    and remembered to be merciful.
For he made this promise to our ancestors,
    to Abraham and his children forever.

—Luke 1:46–55

D o you think you'll ever do it?" my friend asked. She was responding to my confession that someday I hoped to become a writer. I had no definite answer for her. Someday, I thought, the time will come. Someday—it was a typical place to file dreams that rarely come true.

Years later, a small card listing career studies caught my attention in the pile of junk mail. Curious, I checked the box next to "Writer" and mailed the card. Brochures received from correspondence writing schools were carefully filed. It was a step up from the dream file in the back of my mind.

At retirement age, I found myself seeking a purpose for the rest of my life. During one of the many discussions on retirement with my husband, I realized if I were going to pursue writing, now was the time. My heart was loaded with lessons from the Lord, and I wanted to share them to encourage others and make Him known. The Lord confirmed this purpose for me during my search for the reason He had saved my life when I was thrown from a horse several years before.

I felt hopeless, as if I were in a foreign land, trying to communicate something important, while totally ignorant of the language. A brochure from the file of correspondence writing schools was the key that opened the door to learning the craft of writing.

Woven in between the lessons on how to write articles that would sell, I was exposed to the wide world of writing. The vast number of writing genres and markets available was overwhelming. Not only did I need to learn how to write, I had to learn how to sell to an editor to be published. During the course, I wrote stories and articles in different styles, in various categories, and organized in diverse formats. I read through the grammar book, frantically underlining, and came away with the understanding of an alien, but I kept writing. Intimidated by the secular markets, I didn't want to sound too Christian and lost my original purpose. I discovered how little I really knew about the craft of writing.

Like a swimmer out of her depth, I felt like I was floundering. The Lord had to pull me out and set me on the rock of His truth to return my focus to my original objective. I came out of the water soaking wet with self-sufficiency, but once dry, I hopped off the rock and raced down the path of my purpose.

The question "Why am I doing this?" started tiptoeing across my mind. This was taking a long time—precious time that I could be spending with my friends and family. The odds of getting published were not great. When I sat down at my computer, the words didn't fall effortlessly from my fingers as I had imagined. It was hard work. When other writers said things like, "It was years before I got my first book published," and "I could paper my walls with rejection slips," I assumed their words were meant to encourage me, but in reality, I found their comments depressing.

My husband's "tough love" straightened me out and helped me to see God's faithfulness. "If you really love writing, you will sacrifice," he said. "If it's God's purpose, it will be successful." I was grateful for the encouragement. I finished the course and, with certificate in hand, declared, "I am a writer."

Kneeling in prayer, totally dependent on God, the creator of my writing, I felt like a tiny grain of sand on a vast sandy shore. "Lord," I prayed, "I will write what You tell me. Guide me to where You want it published. Give me the courage and perseverance I need to write about Your holiness for generations to come. O Lord, can You provide the things all the writing books insist are necessary? I will need a writer's group, seminars, courses, writing books, a mentor, and people praying for me. I can't see these things happening in my lonely, rural writing room, but you are mighty and have done great things. Amen."

The Lord whispered His answers to my heart. He told me I would often write for ministry and not always for money. He told me my writing was not about me, but for the readers. He told me to pray before each project to be sure it is from Him and not the ugly head of pride surfacing—for He scatters the proud. He also said to listen to the counsel of my husband; that writers need time to think. I knew, in order to do that, I would need to quit my part-time job. I was stunned. My job paid for health insurance and any extras we wanted to enjoy. It was a difficult step of faith, but the Lord has been faithful.

Longingly, I read over the shiny brochure advertising a large writer's conference. It was a fairy tale in the eyes of this novice writer. Our local paper announced that the founder of this conference was going to speak at a local church retreat. *How could this be?* I wondered in amazement. At the retreat, I had the opportunity to speak with her and she put me in touch with local writers also attending. This brought me to a small writer's group in the area and put me in contact with a writer who had worked for the local newspaper. I used the name she gave me and a couple of my articles appeared in the newspaper. I was disappointed when the group disbanded after a few meetings.

In a writer's magazine, I discovered an affordable one-day writer's conference within driving distance that had contests and free critiquing. I soaked up the information taught by published speakers like a sponge and discovered a monthly writer's group in the area. In time, the Lord answered my specific prayer for a second yearly conference.

I began to receive acceptances for some of my stories, articles, and devotions. The power of the Lord has a far reaching and mighty arm. When my articles were edited, I sometimes wondered who actually wrote the published result. However, for me to ignore the assistance of editors would be to deny God's help. I can't do it by myself. Studying the fine-tuning of the professionals has taught me so much.

The Lord satisfied my hunger to express myself by providing inexpensive courses, writer's books and magazines, the opportunity to publish our church newsletter, a faithful group of prayer partners, a mentor, and material for a self-taught course on grammar and punctuation. I am in awe of the tremendous things He continues to provide for me, as I strive to learn more each day about the craft of writing.

I rejoice that He planted the seeds for His purpose in this lowly writer's heart. He cares about the dreams of all who fear Him and works them out in their lives according to His will. He fulfills every promise, and His mercy endures forever.

~Marion E. Gorman

The Day the Sun Came Out

*Christ Jesus, when all is darkness and we feel
our weakness and helplessness, give us the
sense of your presence, your love, and your
strength. Help us to have perfect trust in your
protecting love and strengthening power, so
that nothing may frighten or worry us, for,
living close to you, we shall see your hand,
your purpose, your will through all things.*

—*Ignatius Loyola*

The gray dawn, blanketing my bedroom window
that September morning in 1990, covered my
heart as well. All I could think about was whether or
not I should go on living. Gazing into the dimness,
I reflected on the events that had brought me to this
sorry state.

Seven months earlier, my husband, Norm, our two
teenagers, and I left our home in California and followed two moving vans north to Washington State.
Our plan was to retire in the land of lakes and ever-
greens, where I grew up. It was not an easy decision

to make, as we would be leaving two married daughters behind, but I encouraged myself with the fact that they would be only a short plane trip away.

A week after our arrival, Norm returned to California to "tie up loose ends" at his business. Since our old house remained unsold, he would stay there. That was okay. I had enough to do with unpacking, dealing with a sudden snowstorm, getting my seventeen-year-old Jay and fifteen-year-old Julie into new schools and sewing curtains for the kitchen.

February turned into May. Our old house still hadn't sold, but Norm insisted that it could happen any day. Also, wrapping up those business ends was taking longer than he had thought. Spring turned into summer, and the visits stopped. He no longer returned my calls. I could not reach him by mail. What was going on? A midlife crisis? Another woman? I knew of no way to find out other than to fly to California unannounced. Leaving the kids with my sister, I flew to San Jose. Glad that I still had a key to the old house, I decided to check it out before making a surprise visit to Norm's office. Other than the cot Norm had been sleeping on, the house would be empty, of course. I stepped inside and was shocked.

In the living room was a brand-new couch with matching chair. In the kitchen—an oak dining set and new appliances, including refrigerator. I ran upstairs to find new bedroom furniture and a beautiful flowered comforter on the bed. But it was the note near the phone that brought everything into painful focus. In my husband's familiar handwriting, it read:

"Slim, attractive, single male. If you enjoy candlelight dinners, classical music and walks on the beach, call me." He had composed a singles ad! It would be months before I learned that our "retirement move" had been a carefully orchestrated plan. He would get the wife and kids situated far from home, sprout his wings, and fly free.

I was numb. My husband had never embraced the Christian faith, which made for a difficult marriage, but we had never discussed calling it quits. I drove my rental car to Norm's office, where a surprised secretary ushered me into the inner sanctum. He looked up and smiled.

"You look nice in blue," he said.

"We had better go for coffee," I said.

Once in the booth, he asked when I had received the papers.

"What papers?" I asked.

"The divorce papers."

And there it was. Apparently, divorce papers had been served in Washington while I was flying south. The next days were a blur of tears as I begged my husband to stay in the marriage long enough to finish raising our two youngest kids. But he was resolute, with no reason given except that he was now happier on his own. He returned with me to Washington to gather his belongings.

The kids took it hard. Julie ran away for three days. Jay began hanging out with friends who had purple hair and nose rings. Both experimented with drugs. I was left a single mom with these troubled teenagers. And my dearest friends—any kind of support system at all—were 900 miles away. A rug had been pulled out from under my feet, and I could not regain my balance. That's why, on that gray morning in September, insidious whispers tiptoed into my mind.

"You have failed as a wife. You have failed as a mother. You have failed at life." Never before had I been plunged into a darkness so deep. Never before had I felt so helpless. "Father dear," I prayed. "I cannot see beyond now! All is lost. How can I go on? Help me." But as I sank, a sturdy hand steadied me. Parts of a Scripture verse began to replace my despair with hope. "Though you have made me see troubles, many and bitter . . . you will increase my honor and comfort me once again" (Psalm 71:20, 21 NIV).

Then, it seemed as though God was gently wiping away my tears and reasoning with me. So my husband had left, but other women had survived this catastrophe, and so would I. My kids were in trouble.

They needed me. I had family and loved ones who cared. And most important, for me to give up now simply meant I wasn't trusting God anymore.

With a thankful heart and fresh hope, I got up, took a shower, and slipped into jeans and a pretty yellow sweatshirt. My whole outlook brightened. Instead of forcing down my usual piece of toast, I made pancakes. Then, I told myself that although life was not pretty just now, I could still enjoy pretty things. So, I bought a framed print of peaceful swans on a lake. The next day, I volunteered to work on our church newsletter, and gained new friends. I joined a parent support group and met more.

Today, spring sunshine glows outside my bedroom window and warms my heart as well. Those once troubled teens are married with families of their own, and grandchildren come to visit. With church activities, friends, and too many projects to count, the Lord has given me a life that is full and meaningful.

But when I think back to that gray September morning, I think about others whose circumstances have convinced them that joy has left their lives for good. I want to tell them that trusting in God's loving promises will put them on a road to hope—and give Him the opportunity to show what He can do!

~Karen Strand

Finding Miracles
with Mama

*Lord Jesus, as I enter this workplace, I bring
your presence with me. I speak your peace,
your grace, and your perfect order into the
atmosphere of this office. I acknowledge your
Lordship over all that will be spoken, thought,
decided, and accomplished within these walls.
Lord Jesus, I thank you for the gifts you have
deposited in me. I do not take them lightly,
but commit to using them responsibly and
well. Give me a fresh supply of truth and
beauty on which to draw as I do my job.
Anoint my creativity, my ideas, my energy
so that even my smallest task may bring
you honor. Lord, when I am confused,
guide me. When I am weary, energize
me. Lord, when I am burned out, infuse
me with the light of your Holy Spirit.*

—Prayer for the Workplace

One day, my mother called. "Something strange happened today," she said. "Suddenly I was in the drug store in St. John's and I didn't remember how I got there. I saw my car parked outside and got in and came home."

Our family had already noticed changes in her. She struggled to complete sentences, entered into conversations less frequently, and had become so paranoid of being robbed that her purse swiftly went under a cushion when anyone entered the room.

A trip to the doctor brought the diagnosis of probable Alzheimer's disease. We were told to expect mental deterioration and loss of bodily functions. We also learned she would revert to a childlike state and become bedridden until death ended her downward spiral. Obviously, she could no longer live alone, and my husband and I made the decision to bring her home. It was the beginning of the most difficult, emotionally draining, yet fulfilling, work I've ever done.

I found myself dealing with a range of emotions. Anger—Why did this happen to her? Fear—Where is my mother? I don't even know this person occupying her body. I can't do this. Love—Locked up in this shrunken person is the woman who sacrificed and took care of me when I was little. I want and need to care for her now.

I was overwhelmed by helpless inadequacy. This was my mother. How would I put myself in the place of making decisions for her? How would I deal with the many changes she's undergoing?

My husband, Duane, was entirely supportive, but it wasn't enough. I knew that I had to give her entire care and my involvement in it over to God. Each morning I prayed a prayer of thanks for the opportunity of serving Him by meeting Mama's needs. Difficult and unpleasant tasks continually presented themselves, and I recited the above prayer many times throughout the day.

I also asked God to remind me to look afresh at the beauty of His creation, and daily took time to praise Him. I sat outside, surrounded by His work. Instead of whole trees, each leaf seemed to cry out to be noticed. The lawn no longer resembled a green carpet but, rather, every blade shouted to me of its existence. Tiny pink blossoms on an evergreen shrub, yellow and gold marigolds, red firethorn leaves all persisted in making me aware of their individual presence. I saw God's creation, not as a vast landscape laid down with the artist's hand, but as billions of individual forms, each one well thought out and fashioned, coming together in the picturesque scene before me.

As I praised God for the beauty of each distinct thing I gazed upon, His presence surrounded me and a deep joy filled my soul. In the midst of difficult or mundane tasks, this exercise lifted my spirits. I also asked God to show me how to deal with the changes Mama was going through. Weekly evaluations on her current level of abilities helped me to readjust to her needs and made things easier for me.

Shopping with her went through such an evaluation. Once a pleasant time spent together became increasingly discouraging. She'd sneak things we'd never use into the cart, which I wouldn't discover until we were at the cash register. I would be studying the items coming out of our cart and look up to find Mama gone.

I contacted an Alzheimer's care facility and made arrangements to leave her at the facility for one morning a week. It was the right decision, yet reservations filled my mind as we drove there the first time. Throughout the entire drive, Mama kept asking why I was doing this to her, crying, saying she didn't need to go there. Over and over I gently explained the program and told her she'd enjoy it. She responded to each reassurance by expressing her displeasure and crying. Walking up to the door, I wondered if God had led me in this decision, or if I had been led by my feelings of frustration. She was voicing her unhappiness loudly when the door opened and a smiling woman greeted her. "Hello, Mae."

Mama's contorted expression turned into a wide smile as she said, "Well, hello there." She did enjoy it, and I was able to complete needed errands without aggravation.

Changing what I could enabled me to accept what I couldn't, but nothing stopped the frequency of my frustration. One day, Mama sat at the table watching me decorate a wedding cake. I put the finishing touch to an hour's work on the bottom layer and turned to mix up another batch of frosting. I returned to the table to see a finger in her mouth and a trail running up the side of the cake, through the frosting fleur-de-lis and dropped loops. The whole layer needed to be redone.

"Mama, no," I shouted. Her eyes got big.

I began to pray. OK, Lord, what can I praise You for in this situation? If ever I needed God's peace, it was at that moment. Praising Him in times of exasperation always cleared the path for His peace to envelope me. Lord, I continued, I praise and thank you that the cake didn't fall on the floor and I have plenty of frosting to redo the layer.

Peace replaced my anger. A sheepish smile appeared on Mama's face, and I started to laugh. I ran my finger through the frosting and licked it too. For that moment, I returned to childhood with my mother.

I loved caring for Mama. We held hands when we walked, and Mama put her head on my shoulder while watching television. Our relationship grew closer each day. Yes, there were moments of aggravation and difficulty. Sometimes I failed and reacted in anger. Those times drew me into God's arms. His forgiveness and love filled me, spilling over to my mother.

Mama continued to decline, and I was soon putting in seventeen-hour days caring for her. When she became bedridden, I carefully bathed her, lifted her into a chair, read and sang to her, and fed her. She couldn't say my name, but her beautiful smile met me each time I entered her room.

God's strength allowed me to not only fulfill the responsibilities I once thought impossible, but to find a rich fulfillment in doing them. How glad I was for His presence in the daily activities of my work.

~Dori Clark

The Black Bandana

O! Thou God of all beings, of all
worlds, and of all times,
We pray, that the little differences
in our clothes,
in our inadequate languages,
in our ridiculous customs,
in our imperfect laws,
in our illogical opinions,
in our ranks and conditions which
are so disproportionately important to us
and so meaningless to you,
that these small variations
that distinguish those atoms that we call men,
one from another,
may not be signals of hatred and persecution!

—Voltaire

I lifted a critical eyebrow. My daughter, Sarah,
stood in front of me in black jeans and a black
shirt with a silver studded cross emblazoned across
the front. On her feet were high-heeled black boots.

She ignored my gaze and tied a black bandana in her long brown hair.

"You know, honey," I said, "I think when the group advertised a hoedown, they had more conservative attire in mind. Maybe a long, country skirt, with a red bandana around your neck and a pretty white top would be more appropriate."

She shrugged. "I'm in the mood to wear this."

My stomach clenched. I knew this group. Some of the girls wore only dresses. Most of the kids didn't wear black. Sending my daughter to the party in black from head to toe could cause her to be censured. I opened my mouth to suggest she change, but I felt a check in my spirit and clamped down on my concerns. With a kiss to her cheek and a nagging worry for her emotional well-being, I left for my writer's group's monthly gathering.

Later that evening, as the meeting came to a close, my cell phone rang. I slipped away from the group to take my daughter's call.

"How did it go?"

"It's was hard at first. Everyone stared at me, and I felt as though they thought I was bad. But I just kept smiling and being friendly."

I hung up the phone feeling the pain beneath my daughter's brave words. I also had to push back my own pride. I wanted the adults in that particular community to see me as a godly mother. Did my daughter's wardrobe choices affect their perception of me?

When I returned to the ladies in my meeting, there was a lively conversation going on. The discussion soon turned into a prayer time, and God spoke into our deepest places as we united before Him, sharing our concerns, hopes, fears, hurts, and dreams. Before the impromptu prayer meeting ended, I asked the women if they would pray for my daughter. I shared her experience that night and their mother hearts kicked in, fueling a time of fervent prayer for my feisty, out-of-the-box teenager.

What happened that night turned out to be more about my learning curve than my daughter's needs. As we prayed, God began to reveal to me my daughter's heart, the way He'd created her, and the plans He had for her life. He gently rebuffed me, showing me that my daughter felt undue pressure to conform to a sweet, conservative image that didn't match her personality, or the calling he'd placed upon her.

The Lord then disclosed His irritation toward Christians for getting caught up in our subculture and traditions. It grieved Him that we too often get lost in religiosity, living in self-designed boxes with confining rules that He never intended for us, instead of simply living in a loving relationship with Him and each other.

God showed me that my daughter was following Him—that He planned to use her to stir up Christians who had traded their relationship for Him for traditions. The Lord promised that my daughter would be His instrument to reach the kids who'd never listen to her if she stayed in the safe little box in which we had submerged ourselves.

Then the Lord told me He'd dressed her for the hoedown.

Humbled, I wept before Him and asked Him to make me the mother Sarah needed—the mother who would help her become the woman He wanted her to be.

The next day, Sarah and I had some time alone. I asked her if she ever felt pressure from me to be someone she wasn't. She ducked her head and, carefully, while trying not to hurt me, admitted how often she's experienced the weight of such an attitude.

I apologized and told her I wanted to set her free to follow God as He called. Then I told her about the prayer time and how the Lord had told me that He dressed her for the party.

"That explains it!" Sarah's beautiful green eyes came alive. "What you don't know, Mom, is that, right before the party, I added more makeup and a thick belt to my outfit. I didn't feel rebellious as I did it. I just had this urge to dress my own way instead of how the other kids would.

"It was hard when I first got to the party, but I just kept smiling and being kind, and I think before the evening was over, the kids began to accept me for who I am—to understand that I could be a Christian and not dress like they did. I made several new friends."

I shook my head, chuckling at my young individualist—the adventurous, creative, delightful daughter God had given me. And then I thanked God that she was brave enough to be herself and not let petty differences in dress or culture separate her from other kids who loved Jesus, too.

My teenager is teaching me a lot about looking beyond the outward appearance and truly seeing the heart. As I reflect on this experience, I'm saddened by how often we adults gravitate toward others who look like us, think like we do, and approach life in similar ways.

What would the world look like if we ventured beyond our traditions—our man-made boxes—to embrace those who are different than we are? What if we picked friends from diverse cultures, stations in life, and religious backgrounds? What expansion of understanding might we gain?

I think God must sigh at our petty fears and ridiculous separatist opinions. I wonder if He is whispering something and we're not listening. Could He be telling us that He died on the cross to save mankind, not to set up a religious order where we all look and act alike?

As I dwell on the lesson given me by my fifteen-year-old, I am reminded of the variety of creation. The Creator made more colors than we can label; greater diversity in flora and fauna than anyone has ever captured in all the kingdom, phylum, and classes of our science records; and a bazillion snow-flakes without any two being exactly the same.

May God forgive me for looking at differences and judging His most precious creation, His crowning glory, mankind.

~Paula Moldenhauer

You Promised

Come, you disconsolate, wherever you languish,
come to the mercy seat, fervently kneel.
Here bring your wounded hearts,
here tell your anguish:
earth has no sorrow that heaven cannot heal.
Joy of the desolate, light of the straying,
hope of the penitent, fadeless and pure!
Here speaks the Comforter, tenderly saying,
"Earth has no sorrow that heaven cannot cure."
Here see the Bread of Life; see waters flowing
forth from the throne of God, pure from above.
Come to the feast of love; come, ever knowing
Earth has no sorrow but heaven can remove.

—*Thomas Moore*

I crawled into bed, buried my face in the comfort of my pillow, and pulled the covers over my head. Who cared if it was the middle of the afternoon? I couldn't face another minute of the real world. I had put forth the effort for my entire life, but this was too much. I had to escape.

"Lord," I prayed, "I don't want to question You and Your will, but this is not the way it was supposed to be. I trusted You. That meant You would make everything come out right and it hasn't—this can't be right—it just can't."

My mind rushed back to a day about ten years earlier. "Oh, yes," the orthopedic doctor said, "one other thing. Don't ever have children."

I said nothing. A long discussion was the last thing I wanted. My doctors hadn't spoken of this before, but it was something I already knew. I guess he felt a need to inform me now, since this was my first checkup after my marriage. Hot tears pressed behind my eyelids. Hearing this news from a doctor was like the final drop of a judge's gavel. Instead of hearing a verdict of guilty or not guilty, our judgment was no children, and I was to blame.

For most of my life, I had suffered from a degenerative neuromuscular disease. As I grew up, the disease worsened, and doctors did extensive research. Family histories were taken and different relatives brought in for examination. It turned out to be a hereditary disease.

As a child, that didn't mean much to me other than some other family members had the same thing happening to their bodies to varying degrees. I really didn't care that it was hereditary.

I was too busy coping with doctors, surgeries, and braces.

When I became a teenager, I began to understand more. As far as I was concerned, *hereditary disease* meant two things:

1. Disease—The availability of guys wanting to marry me was going to be small or nonexistent.

2. Hereditary—If I ever did marry, I wouldn't have children.

Those two ideas didn't make me happy. I managed to accept the idea of no children, but I couldn't give up on the idea of having a husband. "I want to marry when I'm forty-two," I told people. I didn't mention my reason—I would be almost past childbearing age by then.

I pictured myself living alone and working in a nearby city. A well-meaning person told my mother, "You should make sure she does secretarial training since she will probably never get married."

Then, something got in the way of those plans. I met a guy—such a special guy—and miracle of miracles, he wanted me. Before long, we started talking about marriage, and I had to tell him about not having children. I was certain he wouldn't want me after my confession. Mike's reaction wasn't rejection, but comfort. He wasn't happy about it, but he still wanted me.

We were married the following winter. Mike and I came to know Christ as Savior and grew in our Christian faith. There was never a dramatic moment of revelation, but somehow, we started to believe we might have children. The idea took hold as we prayed and talked. God was able to overcome the disease. We were certain it was His will for us to start a family. By October, we had our precious baby girl, and another baby girl followed fifteen months later. They were perfectly healthy.

On our oldest daughter's sixth birthday, we went to McDonald's for lunch. As we watched our girls run from one place to another in the play area, my chest tightened in panic. Our oldest daughter was walking and running slightly on her tiptoes, as if her heels wouldn't go all the way down. My last surgery had been to lengthen the tendons in my heels because the disease made them too tight.

"Look at the way she's walking on tiptoe," I breathed.

He watched for a while before answering. "She is, but it's probably okay. Kids goof around a lot."

It wasn't okay. When she continued to walk the same way, we went to an orthopedic doctor. Taking her into that office was like being in one of those nightmares where you try to wake up, but can't. I was the scared little girl again and the heartbroken mother all rolled into one. After a few minutes of examination, the doctor said, "She has the disease."

I couldn't fall apart. I didn't want her to be worried, and no one could predict how the disease would affect her. For a few minutes, I felt like a kid finding out about Santa Claus—confused and slightly betrayed. It didn't matter whether I understood or whether I felt betrayed. God was still real.

She didn't get worse, but we still had regular checkups. My youngest daughter went along to one of those doctor visits. I was already concerned about her, but I kept hoping and trying to deny what I knew was probably true. The doctor asked to look at her feet. It took only a few minutes. "Your younger daughter also has the disease. It's actually worse in her."

That was the day I crawled into bed in the middle of the afternoon. Maybe I would stay there forever. Maybe, I would just die. What was going on here? One daughter might have it, but not both. I pictured lives of struggling through doctor visits and surgeries for my two beautiful little girls. Was life on planet Earth ever fair? I wouldn't blame God; it went against everything I believed. Still, my mind had to hold someone responsible. I turned the guilt to the natural alternative—myself.

I simply got ahead of God. I prayed about having children, and because I wanted them, I convinced myself they would be immune to the disease. I also convinced my husband. Now, they will suffer because I didn't truly hear from God. It's my fault. My family and friends will blame me for my children's pain. Worse still, my children will blame me—rightfully so. My thoughts led me down a wrong path and I followed.

"God, I'm so sorry for trying to have what I wanted without regard for others," I prayed. The sweet peace of forgiven sin did not descend upon me. Days of grief and self-loathing followed. I went through the motions of life, but on the inside I felt like a shattered window with someone knocking out the shards one by one. I went for counseling. It didn't help—nothing helped. My relationship with the Lord ran dry.

I knew what I had to do. On another afternoon I crawled into bed—this time to do battle with myself. "Lord, to the best of my ability I believed that I should have children. I truly believed it to be Your will. If I made a mistake, I'm sorry, but deep in my heart, I know I didn't. I don't understand why my daughters have this disease, but I will accept it. You didn't promise me they wouldn't have it; you promised everything would be okay. So, life is going to be hard. I'm going to wonder every day, week, and year what lies ahead for them, but I choose right now to trust You for however it turns out. I don't understand things the way You do, but I know that You work all things for our good. Whatever happens will be for our good."

Sweet peace flooded over me. I continued to pray, "But, Lord, I am going to pray that You will stop this disease in them and not let it go any further, because I know You have power to do that."

They did have some small problems growing up, but nothing serious. I fought anxiety when they reached their early twenties, because that's when the disease affected my hands. They came through it. At the ages of thirty-one and twenty-nine, they have slightly imperfect feet but happy lives and careers. One has a child.

So, you're thinking, "What if it hadn't turned out so well?" I don't know, but I know God would have shown us the way. I had no strength within myself to overcome the grief or even the desire to conquer it. If I hadn't found strength from the Lord to put the burden of grief on His shoulders, I couldn't have done even that. God has a way of helping us let go.

~*Sandra McGarrity*

Sowing My Seeds
at Wal-Mart

I will go forth to sow my seeds
and every seed that lies
beneath cold winter's eyes
shall take root in God's way.
Kissed by the winds that lightly run
the new blades shall leap to greet the sun.
May the blessing of the earth be on us
the great round earth.
May we ever have a kindly greeting
for people we pass on our way.
And now may the Lord bless
us and bless us kindly.

—An Old Irish Blessing

Feeding and clothing five children requires ingenuity, money, organization, more money, and
lots of trips to Wal-Mart. Most of the time I don't
mind—the thirty-minute drive to and from the store
gives my husband and me the rare opportunity to
be alone together and talk. It may not be my dream

date, but I'll take what I can get. And, even though I love the isolation and solitude of our farm, there are times when I like to get out and mingle with my fellow human beings. Even if those humans are several hundred Wal-Mart shoppers, most of who are talking on their cell phones.

Cell phones aside, I often enjoy the brief interactions I have with the other shoppers. I never miss the opportunity to fuss over a new baby or coax a smile from a toothy toddler. If I see an elderly woman sitting on the bench against the wall, I might stop and visit for a minute. Of course, I don't know a thing about her, but maybe she lives alone and it's been a while since someone asked her how she's doing. And, if I recognize the clerk who checks out our groceries, I try to remember to ask her how her little boy liked his first day of school.

I've never given these fleeting contacts any real significance. Until recently, it never occurred to me that I had the power to make a difference in a stranger's life.

I first met Louise in the customer service department. My husband, Tom, had gone to get a cart and begin grocery shopping while I faced the challenge of returning a few items. I stared bleakly at the line stretching into the main aisle and reluctantly stepped into last place. The minutes passed, and

I began to envy Tom's freedom. I also felt like I had been set up. Tom had simply handed me the bag and said, "Why don't you take this stuff back, and I'll get started on the groceries?" There would be negotiations next time, I vowed as I realized that the line hadn't moved an inch.

Then the woman in front of me dropped her wallet and the contents scattered across the floor. I bent down to help her and, within seconds, she had everything clutched in her hand. When I offered to hold her parcels while she returned the items to her wallet, she flashed a grateful smile. Her trembling hands told me she was flustered, but somehow I knew she was troubled by more than just a dropped wallet. We spent about fifteen minutes in that lineup together, but after a few words of thanks, the woman fell silent.

After I finished serving time in customer service, I went in search of Tom. I found him in the dairy section, and after informing him that I no longer did returns, I told him about the woman and her wallet. "She seemed very nice," I said, "but she wasn't very interested in having a conversation."

He smiled. "Not everyone tells their life story to perfect strangers in lineups," he said in a teasing voice.

"There she is," I said, and nodded toward the

cheese section. Just then, the woman turned around, and our eyes met. I smiled, and to my surprise, she began to walk toward me.

"I just wanted to thank you again for being so kind earlier," she said.

"Oh, that's all right," I replied, and extended my hand. "My name is Susan."

The woman grinned and took my hand with a firm grip. "I'm Louise." The quiet and reserved individual I had met earlier had been replaced with an outgoing and personable woman. Slightly baffled, I listened to her describe her day. When she pointed to our overflowing cart and asked how many children we had, the conversation turned to family. Within seconds, though, her expression lost its animation and, once again, she looked somber and slightly troubled.

Thinking our conversation had ended, I took a step toward our cart where Tom stood, waiting patiently. Abruptly, Louise spoke again. "I have a difficult decision to make," she said. I had no idea what to say, but when she continued talking without waiting for my reply, I realized that she didn't need a response—she needed someone to listen.

She went on to tell me about her grandson, a man in his twenties, who had been living with her for over six months. "He promised me he'd only stay until he got back on his feet," she said. "A few weeks at the most. I have a job, but I can't continue supporting both of us, and he doesn't even look for work. Just sits around all day, watching TV and talking to his friends on the phone."

She paused, and her eyes began to fill with tears. "I decided this morning that I have to tell him to find a new place to stay." She shook her head. "I've been wanting to tell him for quite a while now, but I can never seem to find the courage. I'm not a very brave person."

I tried desperately to think of something to say. It wasn't my place to give her advice, but I wanted to offer some sort of comfort. A very wise lady at church once told me that when you can't think of the right thing to say, ask the Holy Spirit for help, and the words will come to you. So, in a brief silent prayer, I asked for the words I needed, and in what seemed like an instant, I knew exactly what to say. "Oh, but you are brave," I said. "Much braver than you think. I bet you've done a lot of things in your life that took courage."

She nodded slowly. It was as if she had forgotten her moments of bravery and was now just remembering them. "I've been through some rough times," she said. "Dealt with most of it on my own, too."

"Well, I can tell just by talking to you that you're

a strong lady," I said. "And I believe you can do anything you need to do." I paused for a moment. "I'll pray for you."

Louise's beautiful smile returned. "Oh, thank you. That would mean the world to me. You know, I wasn't going to come to the store today. I didn't really need anything, but for some reason, I felt like I had to come." She gave my arm a gentle squeeze. "And now I know why I came. God sent me here to meet you."

Humbled by her gratitude, I could only shrug as if to say, "I didn't do anything special." Then, I noticed Tom looking at his watch. "I'm sorry, but we should get going."

"Me, too," she replied, and we said our goodbyes.

I'd like to see Louise again, sometime. I know she thought that meeting me was a blessing from God, but I'd like the chance to tell her how much she blessed my life in return.

~Susan B. Townsend

Gunnar's Angel

*I look up to the mountains—does my help
come from there?
My help comes from the Lord, who made
heaven and earth!
He will not let you stumble; the one who
watches over you will not slumber.
Indeed, he who watches over Israel never
slumbers or sleeps.
The Lord himself watches over you! The Lord
stands beside you as your protective shade.
The sun will not harm you by day, nor the
moon at night.
The Lord keeps you from all harm and
watches over your life.
The Lord keeps watch over you as you
come and go, both now and forever.*

—Psalm 121:1–8

Jennifer's fearful voice cut in and out over her cell phone. "Mom, Gunnar's been run over. Life-Flight's taking him to Children's Mercy downtown."

"Where are you? Why aren't you with him in the helicopter?"

"There wasn't room for us. He needs someone there when he gets to the hospital. Please hurry."

I glanced at the alarm clock and calculated the time it would take she and Scott to drive the forty-five miles from Paola, Kansas, to the hospital. My mind ran over her words again and again as I stumbled out of bed, looked for some clothes, and scrambled to find a pair of shoes. *Is this a dream? No. This must be real. How could this happen? Did she say he had been run over? Is he all right? Where were they this time of night?* The questions continued to bombard me while I pointed my car toward downtown Kansas City on I-35 from suburban Overland Park, Kansas.

Unfortunately, my husband, Vic, was out of town—I would have to go this one alone. *Help me, Father God, to be strong even though he isn't here.* I fought back unthinkable images as I drove, but they continued. *What will I find when I get there? I wonder if he's conscious. He must be hurting so.* I turned my fears into prayers. *Father God, bless Gunnar. Keep him and his family calm. Give the doctors wisdom.*

While I drove, I remembered the half-hour trip to the blueberry patch that morning. My prayers, then, had centered on Jennifer and her family. Just the memory of that prayer time brought peace to me. No matter what I found when I got to the hospital, I had a quiet confidence, knowing Jesus was in charge, no matter what. I focused on that fact and began to praise Him for His provision.

I pulled into the deserted parking lot and made my way to the emergency entrance. The charge nurse looked up from her paperwork. "May I help you?"

"I'm here for Gunnar Karr."

"Are you family?" she asked.

"I'm his grandmother."

"Wait here. I'll page them inside the exam room to let them know you're here," she said as she picked up the phone.

While I waited, I kept up the prayers. *Father, no matter what I see, don't let me show alarm to Gunnar. Stand between him and the pain. Keep him from fear.*

Soon, a lady paramedic came out of the emergency exam room with a transport basket under her arm. "Are you Gunnar Karr's grandmother?" she asked.

"Yes."

"Well, so far the X-rays show no broken bones. They'll take him for a CT scan soon to check for internal injuries. You'll be able to see him in just a minute. He's quite calm. In fact, he fell asleep in the helicopter on the way in."

I blinked hard, trying not to cry. "Oh, thank you. Is there a phone I can use to call his mom and dad?"

She pointed to a wall phone. "Just dial 9 to get out."

While the phone rang, another barrage of questions pelted me. *Did she say "No broken bones?" How could a car run over a five-year-old and not break bones? Maybe Jennifer was exaggerating. Maybe she just thought the car ran over him.*

"Jennifer. We have good news. No broken bones. They'll take him in for CT scans in a minute."

"Have they let you see him yet?" she asked. I could hear the apprehension in her voice. "Not yet. They said soon." I hung up the phone. I marveled that Gunnar had fallen asleep in the helicopter. *Father, thank You for calming Gunnar.*

A nurse came out of the exam room. "You can see him now."

Gunnar was a heartbreaking sight. He lay very still. They had cut off all his clothes. A white plastic neck brace held his head still. There was no question he had been run over. Two dirty black tire marks ran across his little five-year-old frame from his left hip to his right shoulder. He looked so small and helpless as he lay on that big exam table with a huge bright light overhead. I took his hand and brushed his hair back from his forehead.

"Two tires ran over me, Grandma," he whispered.

"I know, honey. Your mom told me. Mom and Dad will be here soon."

The doctors prodded and poked his tiny frame. He cried out only when they rolled him on his side. The only injuries I could see were a few scrapes on his knees and one on his right hip.

Jen and Scott arrived while Gunnar was in the CT scanner. Jennifer's shaking hand reached out for mine. I hugged her, and we took a seat in the waiting room. "So, fill me in," I said. "What happened?"

"We were at Jordan's baseball game at the fairgrounds. Gunnar was playing on the swing sets across the street behind the bleachers. I heard a thump behind me, and I turned around just in time to see a limp body fly out from behind a midsized car. I jumped down and ran to the kid in the street. I couldn't believe my eyes. It was Gunnar. He was so still. I didn't know if he was dead or alive."

I handed her a tissue. "Who was the driver?"

"A fifteen-year-old kid in a borrowed car. He stopped a few feet down the street. Someone called Med-Act, and they got there pretty quick. While the EMTs worked on him, some guy came out of the crowd and knelt at Gunnar's feet and prayed."

"Who was it?"

"Don't know. Never saw him before."

"Well, what did he look like?"

"Couldn't see his face. His ball cap hid it. He had overalls on. When Gunnar cried out in pain, the man prayed even louder."

"That's strange. Were the emergency people upset about him being there?" I asked.

"That's the weird part. They never said a word to him." Jennifer blew her nose. "Just kept working. Like he wasn't even there. Before too long the Life-Flight helicopter arrived and took off with Gunnar. I turned to thank the man who prayed for him, but he was gone. I asked several people about him. No one knew him."

I shook my head. "That's weird. Everybody knows everybody in Paola."

A doctor entered the waiting room. "Mrs. Karr?"

"Yes."

"We can't find any internal injuries, but we better keep Gunnar for observation. We have a room ready for him upstairs."

"Can I stay with him?"

"Sure. We'll do further tests in the morning."

That next morning Gunnar couldn't sit up or walk. All through Saturday, the doctors ordered test after test, with no conclusive diagnosis. By Sunday, word of his accident had spread to many church congregations in Paola, Overland Park, and beyond.

Every doctor who examined Gunnar came up

with a different reason why he couldn't sit up or walk. One doctor thought Gunnar might have a hairline crack in his pelvis. Further tests showed there were no cracks. Another doctor thought that a body cast from his neck to his knees for two months would be the best treatment. Still another suggested his growth plate might be damaged. If this were the case, Gunnar would never grow taller than three feet nine inches.

After two days and nights of never leaving his side, Jennifer was in tears after each doctor's visit. She called me in the depths of despair on Monday. My heart went out to her as she sobbed, "Mom, I can't take any more of this. Every doctor has a different plan of treatment. What should we do? Which one is right?"

"Jennifer, we're going to trust the Lord. His wisdom is greater than ours. His hand is in this." I hesitated for a moment and then continued. "I'm not so sure the guy with the ball cap and overalls wasn't an angel."

She said nothing for a few seconds. "I think you might be right, Mom." We ended our conversation by praying that the Lord would take the whole situation into His hands.

To everyone's surprise, that afternoon, Gunnar sat up for the first time, with no pain, and in a couple of hours, he could stand and take a few steps. On Tuesday morning, physical therapists fitted him with a tiny walker. After a few minutes' instruction, he managed to walk down the hall. He looked so funny—like a little old man. That afternoon, the hospital discharged him. On the way to the car, Gunnar lifted the walker over his head like a barbell.

"Gunnar, for heaven's sake," I said. "Put that walker on the ground and use it like you've been told. If the doctors see that kind of thing, they might not let you go." Gunnar flashed me one of his wide, dimpled grins.

Wednesday was the Fourth of July. Gunnar parked his walker permanently and celebrated Independence Day by running in the yard for hours. I honored the day and my Lord by silently giving thanks to the One who heard and answered our prayers.

~Sally Jadlow

Homeless in Seattle

May I become at all times,
both now and forever
A protector for those without protection
A guide for those who have lost their way
A ship for those with oceans to cross
A bridge for those with rivers to cross
A sanctuary for those in danger
A lamp for those without light
A place of refuge for those who lack shelter
And a servant to all in need.

—Anonymous

He looked like any other homeless man wandering the streets of Seattle that sunny afternoon in September; with his disheveled hair, ankles exposed beneath a pair of too-short pants, oversized sweatshirt covered with stains and the smells to go with them, and ratty old sneakers. He approached my husband, Donald, and me where we sat in the sunny fresh air of the waterfront, enjoying a day of sightseeing in the city.

His desperate plea sounded familiar. "Could you spare a few dollars? I haven't eaten since breakfast." He seemed sincere, but we were skeptical. I wanted to help, but I hate being put on the spot. Sensing my reaction, Donald told him, "No. Sorry, no."

As he walked away, we couldn't shake the feeling of compassion we felt for this young man. "Everybody has a story," my husband pointed out.

"Yep, that's right."

"Do you think I should find out his?"

I nodded. "Sure, why not?"

Donald caught up to the young man. After listening for a few minutes, he returned to our table.

"He said he came down here from Alaska to work on a fishing boat. The job fell through, and two days later, his wallet was stolen along with every piece of his identification. He has spent the past month trying to find someone to help him regain his identity. It seems no one wants to help him."

As I let the news digest, he added, "Let's take him to lunch. I have a feeling about this kid."

Soon we were sitting outside Ivar's with Tony, munching on fish and chips while the seagulls circled overhead begging for a bite.

"So, Tony, how is it you came to be homeless?" I asked. Tony told the same story Donald had related to me. "What about a church?" I probed. "There has got to be somebody who can help you."

"Well, I was turned away at the mission because they require ID for any male to enter the facility. I've been on the streets since July and even celebrated my twenty-first birthday sleeping on a park bench. All I need is a new birth certificate and Social Security card, but no one will help me."

Donald and I looked at each other. "We'll help you, Tony," Donald said. "Write down all your information: your parents' names, your birth date, and place of birth. We'll send for your birth certificate."

Before we left Tony that day, we joined hands in prayer. "Lord, keep your hands on Tony. Encourage him today and continue to protect him, heavenly Father. Guide us in helping him and above all, may he realize the depth of Your love for him, Lord. In Jesus's name we pray, Amen."

"Thank you." Tony's eyes grew moist. "No one has tried to help me since I've been here."

"I hope you know how much God loves you," I said.

"Oh, yes, believe me, I do."

We left Seattle feeling hopeful. On Monday, however, we ran into a roadblock in applying for Tony's birth certificate. We asked for prayer about the situation during our weekly Bible study, and one of the women in our group who works for the Social Security Administration gave us some encouraging information.

"He doesn't need a birth certificate to get a copy of his SS card. If he can obtain a transcript from the high school he attended or something from a former employer showing any identifying information, he can get his Social Security card. Persistence is the key. Tell him to let the clerks at the Social Security office know that he is willing to do whatever it takes to get his card."

One of our main obstacles to helping Tony was finding him again. He told us he was staying in a "tent city" that had been set up behind a church. We tried calling this church several times to relay a message to Tony, but he never received any of our notes. Consequently, we planned a trip up to the shelter.

Saturday morning, we prepared a packet of information that would help Tony in regaining his identity. As much as we wanted to help him, we also wanted Tony to help himself. We included the forms he needed to apply for his birth certificate, some postage-paid envelopes, a calling card and phone numbers for the Driver's License Office and Social Security Administration, as well as a written account of everything we had learned that week that might help him in his quest. Finally, the most precious part of the packet was a Bible, the Word that could truly help him find his way.

Donald and I prayed and talked during the forty-five-minute drive to the tent city, and we placed our worries and concerns into God's capable hands. As we turned the corner beside the church and approached the parking area, we could see a small lot covered with tents mostly made out of blue tarps. Incredibly, in front of it all sat a desk under a makeshift shelter. We hesitantly approached this muddy reception area and were greeted by a friendly middle-aged man, wearing a dark stocking cap and an Army jacket.

"We're here to see Anthony Beenken," Donald announced.

"Let me see," the man said as he skimmed down a list of names on a clipboard. "Ah, here he is. Anthony is in 'Hilton One.'"

Donald and I looked at each other with surprise. Hilton, huh? They have some sense of humor, I thought as I scanned the meager surroundings that were home to dozens of people. Another man went to check in "The Hilton."

"He's not there. He must be gone for the day," he said when he returned.

We left the folder with the man in charge of the shelter and left the entire situation with God, the

One who is truly in charge. Then, we climbed in our car and headed home.

Tony called later that day. Over the next few weeks, he stayed in touch and even attended church with us one Sunday. He enjoyed it immensely, singing all the praise and worship songs. Obviously, this was a young man who knew the Lord.

"So, when did you come to know Christ as your Savior?" I asked Tony over fried chicken and potato salad at the church fellowship dinner.

"Oh, several years ago at a Promise Keeper's convention."

I learned how he had read the entire Bible several times, something I certainly could not claim for myself. His family was broken; his mother was in jail for drugs, his father died when he was three, his younger siblings were in foster care, and his older sister's location was unknown. He told us about his love for animals and how, as a young child, he would bring home all the strays in the neighborhood until his house was overflowing with cats and dogs.

Later the following month, Tony was nearly kicked out of the tent city for failing to solicit a $25 gift card from any local store to help raise money for the facility. On the day before he was to be evicted, my daughter and I paid him a visit and found him feeling discouraged and dejected. "I can't survive out there. I can't even carry all my stuff. It's dangerous and it's getting colder. I'll be dead within days."

"Don't give up, Tony," I replied. "God is bigger than this problem. Keep praying and resting in the knowledge that He loves you and cares for you."

"I know, but sometimes it seems like my prayers are falling on deaf ears."

"Well, that's because we can't see the big picture. But God has a reason for you to go through this time of difficulty. Hang in there, Tony," I said, and we left.

Even though Tony needed only $25, I felt strongly that God didn't want me to just write a check and solve his problem. No, the Lord had something else in mind. The next day I asked for prayer in church, explaining Tony's predicament. After the service, a woman approached me in the fellowship hall.

"I want to donate a gift card to Tony," she said.

I wasn't surprised. I knew God would come through. We took the card up to tent city that afternoon, handing it to the man behind the desk.

"This is for Anthony Beenken," I said.

"He's sure going to be glad to see this," the man said with a big smile. "He was so distraught last night. He's not here right now; he's still at church, but we will make sure he receives credit for this. God is always coming through for us around here. Things seem to come out of the woodwork at just the right time."

A few weeks later, our family moved across the country to South Carolina. Even though we lost touch with Tony, I know that this is not the end of his story. There are many more chapters to be written because God has a special plan for his life. I hope when Tony looks back on this difficult time, it will encourage him to continue living in the faith that grew through answered prayer. I hope he will continue to believe that anything is possible with God. Finally, I hope that he will pass on the love of God that he has experienced to everyone he meets.

~*Cindy Boose*

The Mother I Long to Be

Creator of all things, true source of light and
wisdom, origin of all being,
graciously let a ray of your light penetrate
the darkness of my understanding.
Take from me the double darkness
in which I have been born,
an obscurity of sin and ignorance.
Give me a keen understanding,
a retentive memory, and
the ability to grasp things
correctly and fundamentally.
Grant me the talent
of being exact in my explanations
and the ability to express myself
with thoroughness and charm.
Point out the beginning,
direct the progress,
and help in the completion.
I ask this through Christ our Lord.
Amen.

—St. Thomas Aquinas

I grabbed my purse and car keys and headed out the door to pick up my son from elementary school. I smiled as I remembered his excitement that morning about dressing up just like his daddy. It was picture day at his school, and he had pleaded with me to buy him a tie. That morning I buckled his belt, straightened his clip-on tie, and combed his hair. "Now are you sure you know how to unbuckle your belt?" I asked him.

"Watch this, Mom!" he replied, while demonstrating his ability with confidence.

"Way to go, buckaroo!" I laughed. "You look amazing!"

Driving to school that afternoon, I thanked God for the joy found in parenting. This joy was a welcome visitor because, too often, I felt overwhelmed by the challenges of motherhood.

Growing up in an abusive home had left me haunted by the fear of doing the same to my own children. My mother was the child of an abusive alcoholic and continually struggled with fits of rage and violence while trying to raise her three children. She died when I was seventeen, and although I loved her, it was the first time I felt safe. As I approached adulthood, I vowed never to have children, determined to end the cycle of abuse. Years later, after surrendering my life to God,

I discovered that my plans were not necessarily God's plans.

Marrying my husband and giving birth to my son was my first step of faith toward conquering the fear that had plagued me. God gave me grace daily as my son matured and I became pregnant again. One child was manageable, but the thought of two children to care for aroused my old insecurities. With another baby on the way, I knew I would need more help. I read countless books on parenting, attended counseling sessions to deal with my past issues, and received tremendous support from my husband. Still, I wrestled with insecurity and battled the fear that, with added responsibility, I would follow in the abusive pattern of my mother.

I pushed all these thoughts aside as I climbed the steps of my son's school. Usually I picked up my son in the front hallway, but today his teacher politely redirected me to the library. I entered the room and, right away, I immediately sensed something was wrong. My son stood in the rear of the room. His head hung down, and he clutched a book close to his body. I drew closer, smelled a foul odor, and immediately knew what had happened. He had gone to the bathroom in his pants. He raised his head when I called his name, and I saw the horror of embarrassment in his eyes. His lips quivered and tears began to fall. "Mommy, I couldn't unbuckle the belt," he whispered. "I tried so hard, but it was too late."

I was suddenly overwhelmed with memories from my own childhood. I remembered the time I had soiled my pants at the dentist's office because of nerves; my mother yelled and later beat me. Another time I spilled milk all over my new dress and spent hours in the closet to avoid a beating. I recalled cringing in fear every time I made a mistake or failed in some way. The waves of shame I encountered as a child were now mirrored in the face of my young son.

I realized quickly that I didn't know how to respond to my son. I knew what would be an inappropriate response, but there was a gaping hole in my mind concerning how I should properly handle this situation. What was I to do? I felt a lump in my throat and my palms began to sweat. I searched the room for help, but we were all alone. One part of me wanted to run and hide; another part of me genuinely longed for an answer. What was I to do? To whom could I turn?

Even before I could finish my question the answer came. *Turn to Me.* It was a quiet voice, but one I recognized. It was the voice that comforted me as a child traumatized from abuse and the same voice that pleaded with me as an adult to forgive my mother. I cleared my throat and whispered the name of Jesus in a desperate plea for help. Suddenly, I knew what to do.

Kneeling down, I embraced my son and reassured him of my love for him. I wiped away his tears of shame and asked how his classmates had treated him. Surprisingly, I discovered only his teacher was aware of his problem. She had met him at the bathroom door, promptly escorted him to the rear of the library, and reminded him that I would soon arrive. I swiftly wrapped his jacket around his waist, positioned his lunch box in front of his hips, and instructed him to stay close to me.

"B-but, Mommy," he stammered, "what about the smell?"

"Don't worry," I whispered with a grin, "everyone will think it's me!"

We both giggled at the thought. Walking down the corridor to exit the building, I continued to remind him that the people we passed were most certainly thinking that I was to blame for the foul smell. His giggles turned to laughter that persisted all the way to the car. I grabbed an extra plastic bag I had in the car and laid it on the seat for my son. "Sir, you may be seated, but please forgive my poor taste in choices of perfume!" I joked while my son roared with laughter.

During the drive home, my son began to discuss the rest of his day. In the midst of his chatter, I realized that he was no longer concerned about his problem. He was just enjoying being with his mom. A tear slid down my cheek as God revealed to me the miracle that had taken place. I realized that I had taken my son's shame on myself and carried it down that school hallway. I protected him from the pain of humiliation by allowing myself to be humbled in his place. Once again, I heard that soft, comforting voice. *As I did for you.* "Yes, Lord," I said under my breath, "just like You did for me on Calvary."

It was then I grasped the true miracle of God's love. At that moment, I understood the desire of God's heart to calm my fears and erase my doubts. He would guard me and keep me. I knew that if I trusted Him to help me, I would be the mother I longed to be.

~*Ginny Caroleo*

Whatsoever Things
Are Lovely

And now, dear brothers and sisters, one final
thing. Fix your thoughts on what is true, and
honorable, and right, and pure, and lovely,
and admirable. Think about things that
are excellent and worthy of praise.

—*Philippians 4:8*

Even the rain beating against the windshield of the car couldn't dash my spirits as I drove home from the Cancer Center. I sang along with the mellow music that was playing on the car radio, my heart bursting with the joy of celebration. Four years, almost to the day, after my surgery, the doctor had smiled and said, "In five years, Mrs. Hewitt, you should be cancer free. You will continue to need a blood test every six months, and another colon scope in three years, but everything right now looks good." The words of the old gospel hymn, "This is my story; this is my song, praising my savior all the day long," drifted across my mind.

A crisis often brings an opportunity for self-reflection. As a result of having this disease, I can't help but sometimes worry about my future. I am still fearful and anxious, but it's then I seek God's presence and try to take my life one day at a time. Instead of wondering how I will get through the week or the month, I try to focus on today. That's not always easy—on the great weaving loom of life, the threads of yesterday are inextricably woven into the ones of today.

Four years ago, my husband and I sat in the gastroenterologist's office, trying to read the doctor's face as he leafed through my case file on his desk. The biopsy report stated that I had cancer of the colon. The words pierced my heart, which was beating in a frantic rhythm. His voice droned on, discussing my immediate future, and scheduling an appointment with a surgeon, while my brain raced and I rubbed my sweaty palms. Where was God in all of this?

Somewhat calmer, we left the doctor's office to drive home. It was autumn in Ohio, a spectacular season of yellow- and red-leafed maple and elm trees. It was a time of harvest, and the fields were filled with fat orange pumpkins. The orchards offered their bounty of apples, ready for picking. Through tear-filled eyes, I watched this panorama fast forward through the car windows until, at last, we reached our driveway.

It was then I saw it—the old sassafras tree in our back pasture as the sun glimmered through its branches. It stood resplendent, as it had for many years, in its robes of gold. I remembered it would soon be Thanksgiving, and words of praise filled my heart. "Thank you, God, for your wondrous world," I whispered. Facing major surgery, I realized I could lose my life. Faith, as I understood it, meant that I had to trust in God even when I didn't know the outcome. With God's help, I could handle whatever happened. He was in control. This was His world, and my faith in Him was my anchor. Remembering the loveliness of the sassafras tree and meditating on the words of Scripture, "whatsoever things are lovely," sustained me in the coming weeks.

When we visited the surgeon's office, he was efficient and professional as he explained the procedure, the possible outcome, and what my options might be. "He probably has performed this type of surgery many times," my husband said in an effort to reassure me. I liked the surgeon and felt I could trust him. It wasn't until my hospital pre-op session with the hospital health professionals that I fell apart.

Our daughter who lives three hundred miles away was coming to be with me during the surgery.

When I called her to tell her about my pre-op experience, she said, "Mother, why did you go alone?" I told her that there didn't seem to be anyone available, and I didn't know what I would encounter. The nurse who gave me my instructions was capable and kind. She explained what would be happening on the actual day of the operation, how I should prepare for the surgery, the anesthetic they would use, what they could do to alleviate pain, and all the details of the recovery room. My pulse raced as all this data crowded my senses. For the first time, I was aware of the enormity of my situation.

That night, I awoke in a cold sweat as panic smothered me like the hot waves shimmering from the steamy pavement on a blistering summer day. I was unable to sleep, but I felt the nearness of God. "God," I whispered, "give me a sign that everything is going to be all right." My heartbeat slowed and I slept.

The next morning, I was awakened by a call from a nurse friend living in Florida. "Who is your doctor?" she asked in a cheery voice. When I told her, she said, "Oh, he is the same one I worked with for a year before I retired. He is a fine surgeon, an excellent Christian doctor, and a kind and caring man." Janice's words and the words from Scripture, "whatsoever things are of good report, think on these things," assured me the Lord had heard my plea. When I finally entered the operating room, I knew God would be there beside me, along with the hundreds of prayers of loving Christian friends and family.

I was in the operating room for six hours, and after talking with the doctor, my family knew I needed rest and prepared to leave. With my family circling my bed in thankful prayer, our son asked God to surround me with watchful angels through the night. I pushed my morphine pump after they said their good-byes, and slept.

Toward dawn, I awoke to see a radiant light and brightly lit face peering down at me. In an instant it was gone. My heart began to race. What had I seen? Were the drugs causing me to hallucinate? I began to observe the faces of every nurse and hospital aide, anyone that might have been bending over me in my dark room. No one resembled the face I saw.

That was four years ago, and I still feel God's healing presence with me. I am still unsure of what I saw that night alone in my hospital room, but after months of recovery, I am sure of one thing. I was seriously ill and now I am well. I believe that God does send His ministering angels to watch over us. God loves and cares for us, and He speaks to us in myriad ways, if we stop and listen. He has been patient as I have tried to make time to be silent and to pray. It is difficult for me to be quiet, but I am learning to sit in my garden each morning and pay attention to God.

My cancer was found in its early stages, and I have recovered, at least for the present. My doctor told me that I wouldn't be declared cancer-free for five years, and I have one more year to go. This event in my life has taught me that we can expect the promises of God to help us cope, no matter what our situation might be.

These days I find so many ways to be thankful, and I try to focus on life's small wonders. For me, faith is not only a deeply felt comfort, but also the only path to a meaningful life.

When I was at the lowest point in my health crisis, I cried out, "Where is God in all of this?" I no longer have to wonder, because I know, now, that He was with me through it all.

~Betty Jane Hewitt

The Promise of Hope

*Relieve and comfort, Lord, all the persecuted
and afflicted. Speak peace to troubled con-
sciences, strengthen the weak, confirm the
strong, instruct the ignorant, deliver the
oppressed from him that oppresses him, and
relieve the needy that have no helper. Bring
us all, by the waters of comfort and in the
ways of righteousness, to the kingdom of rest
and glory; through Jesus Christ, our Lord.*

—Jeremy Taylor

In 2002, I felt bored with my life and circumstances. Because of my vision problems and my
wait for a second cornea transplant, my life had
boiled down to work, cook, clean, and fall into bed
exhausted.

Years before, I had been involved with church
ministry groups. Now in my forty-third year of marriage, I felt as though I'd been put on a shelf. If
I complained aloud, my husband, Gary, reminded me
of my Christian influence at work, and how much

our children and grandchildren relied on my prayers. I knew my prayers had value; still, I desired a broader mission field.

If anyone read my journal, they would sense my fear and insecurity. One note says, "No money. Looks like we'll work until we we're seventy." Nothing seemed to change the first eight months of that year, other than Gary's biceps grew smaller and his belly bigger. "Hon, please leave the doughnuts alone," I begged him.

"Mook." He called me the nickname he'd given me years before. "I'm an old man. Old men get paunchy, you know."

One steamy afternoon in August, when I arrived home from work, Gary met me at the back door. "Mook, what do you think about me applying for early retirement?"

"How on earth do you think we'd pay the bills?" My heated anger seemed to warm the kitchen. After the initial blowup, we didn't discuss the idea again, but I didn't sleep well. I woke up feeling the need to apologize and decided a written apology might help. I searched for paper and finally reached into a card box, took the card on top, and wrote, *"Darling Husband, you are worth more than a hundred grand to me. We will survive. We always have. Retire man! Retire—Love, Mook."*

Before I placed the card in Gary's lunch pail, I read Isaiah 58:11, praying, "Lord, will he think I'm trying to manipulate him? I'm not. If you want him to retire, I'll trust you."

I read my note once more and flipped the card over to read the verse again, *The Lord will guide you always.* With that, I put the card in his lunch pail and left for work.

In November, I received my second transplant and, three weeks later, the doctor pronounced the surgery successful. The next morning Gary called me at work. "Mook, make an appointment for me to see the doctor." I thought my jokester husband was teasing me. He hated illness and had not seen a doctor in seven years. In the next few days, I realized how self-focused I'd been with my vision. The larger-than-life belly Gary sported was a problem that couldn't be solved with a larger pair of pants.

The doctor made light of the problem, ordered some blood work, and said he'd call. Before the lab report returned, we had rushed Gary to the ER. The doctor told me he suspected cancer.

The next morning, a radiologist performed a paracentesis and drained four liters of gelatin-like fluid from Gary's abdomen, allowing him relief. Our doctor called in a surgeon.

After surgery, the doctor said, "Your appendix

had burst and there are hundreds of little tumors everywhere. I've never seen anything like this, but I researched your condition. You have a rare disease, mucinous cystadenoma with pseudomyxoma peritonei (PMP)." She explained more, and then added, "I've called in an oncologist."

The oncologist, whom my husband later dubbed "Dr. Death," gave us no hope. "Unfortunately, there is no treatment," he said. When we pressed for an idea of what we might expect, he said, "He might live three days, or three weeks, or three months. We don't know."

Later Gary jogged my memory back to August. "Mook, I didn't know about the cancer then, but the verse you sent in my lunch became my promise of hope. Please bring it to me."

When I returned and handed Gary the card, he read aloud, "The Lord will guide you always; he will satisfy your needs in a sun-scorched land and will strengthen your frame. You will be like a well-watered garden, like a spring whose waters never fail" (NIV).

"Mook," he said, "pray that no matter what happens next, whether I live or die, that God will receive the glory."

In the next few days, while Gary slept, I silently prayed. "Lord, comfort my husband, and touch his afflicted body." I felt confused. "Father, I don't know how to pray. I'm selfish, and beg you to let my husband live, yet I hate to see him in pain." Finally I added, "Thy will be done on earth as it is in heaven, and as Gary requested, You receive the glory in everything."

That first hospital stay became the first of many struggles. Two days after surgery, the doctors thought Gary might not live through the weekend. Our children flew from Oregon to Nebraska to share their dad's last hours. Gary rallied, and thirteen days later, we took him home. Less than a month after surgery, his abdomen ballooned again. We chose a different hospital and a new set of oncologists. After two weeks of testing and another paracentesis, Gary returned home. Later, the oncologist called me at work. "If you have family medical leave, take it now. You won't have him much longer."

Yet Gary lived.

The longer he lived, the more I studied the Isaiah 58 passage, not just the eleventh verse, but also the promises of the whole chapter. I poured out my feelings in a journal. "Help Lord, my whole life hurts," I wrote, while I figured out ways to restructure our debt load and to encourage my husband to write out a power of attorney, a health power of attorney, and make out a will.

Three months after his diagnosis, I found myself listening to Gary sleep. While he snored, I prayed. If he didn't snore, I'd check his body to see if he'd died.

In May, Gary returned to the hospital for another paracentesis. While there, he asked the doctor if he could fly to Oregon to see family and friends. We made the journey armed with medical notes and the oncologist's cell phone number. "Keep these close," the oncologist instructed. "If an emergency arises, chances are the doctors won't recognize your rare cancer, or know how to treat you in crisis."

While in Oregon, Gary refused to talk about his illness. While he pretended life was normal, I shared his condition with everyone. Two women gave me information on a vegan diet that might make a difference.

We were gone ten days and returned home without incident, but soon, Gary returned to the hospital for another paracentesis. Afterward, he suffered excruciating pain and weakness. His recliner became his haven, where he slept for three days. While he slept, I studied the nutrition suggestions.

"Lord, is it possible the diet and all that carrot juice might help?"

Gary agreed to try the vegan diet for six weeks. The first week, he gained remarkable strength. He continued on the strict raw diet with sixty-four ounces of carrot juice daily. Over the next few months, he developed a navel hernia, but worked in the yard, built picture frames, and remodeled some of our house.

Eleven months after Gary's diagnosis, nausea consumed me until I couldn't see the computer screen to work. "Lord, give me peace while you continue your work in our

circumstances." Tears threatened. "God, Gary's cancer has helped me see how fear rules my life. Forgive me, Lord." Peace came.

Then, miraculously, we learned about a PMP cancer clinic only four miles from our home. A year after his no-hope, no-treatment diagnosis, Gary consulted with Dr. Brian Loggie at Creighton Cancer Center. He showed us CT scans from the first surgery to the present, and said it appeared the nutrition had reduced the tumors and given Gary the strength to undergo surgery. He then explained the intraperitoneal hypothermic chemotherapy (IPHC) surgery treatment, a heated chemo wash, and the possibility he would need to remove some organs.

After a nine-hour surgery, Dr. Loggie grinned and reported, "I do believe I've seen a miracle. I think we got every tumor."

Two years before, I'd complained about our small world where I felt useless. After the IPHC surgery, and Gary's months of healing, our world broadened to a worldwide mission field. We are a part of a PMP support group, and I write for the caregivers' corner on the PMP Web site, *www.pmpawareness.org.*

Only the Lord knows how long Gary will live. When people talk about his rare cancer, he says, "I had a rare cancer. The Lord healed me." He now works in a bakery, where he rubs shoulders with hundreds of people who we add to our prayer list.

Daily we pray, "Lord, comfort the afflicted, and in everything may you receive the glory. We praise you. Amen."

~Katherine J. Crawford

Partners in Prayer

Thank you for the world so sweet.
Thank you for the things we eat.
Thank you for the birds that sing.
Thank you, God, for everything.

—*Child's Prayer of Thanks*

My son Josiah flung open the screen door and careened into my open arms. I embraced him and finally exhaled. I had waited seven and a half excruciating hours to hear about his first day of fourth grade.

"Mommy, I had fun today," he announced.

"That's great, sweetheart." I chuckled and allowed his enthusiasm to flow around me. "Now tell me all about it."

He led me into the living room and proceeded to do just that, in great detail. As he gushed on and on about old classmates, new students, and his new teacher, I silently prayed that this school year would not mirror the previous one—with one exception.

I asked that Josiah's budding faith could continue to blossom via the vehicle of prayer.

Over the past year, Josiah had discovered the joy of praying for his own needs and those of others. "I'll pray for you," he'd volunteer upon hearing distressing news from family and friends. Sometimes he tabled the requests for later so that we could petition God together. Other times he would boldly—and immediately—pray. Either way, he never forgot to pray once he had promised to do so. No request was too large or too small. Josiah eagerly prayed for *everything*—from his grandmother's recovery, to his uncle's lost job, to his cousin's horrific car accident. Josiah prayed, expected answers, and kept praying.

Ironically, it had been prayer that initially watered his faith.

The night before Josiah entered third grade, we concluded our evening bedtime ritual with a prayer I uttered at the beginning of each new school year. "Lord," I prayed, "please give Josiah the best teacher for *him*. She doesn't have to be the best teacher in the school, just the best for him." Josiah echoed my "Amen" before falling asleep full of eager anticipation for the new school year.

That excitement paled as the first quarter unfolded. The third-grade curriculum was more rigorous than Josiah expected, and then my mother—who provided care for him before and after school—became ill and had to be hospitalized twice. In addition, Josiah was still missing his many friends from our former church, which we had left a few weeks before the school year started. The more he fretted about Grandma and missed his friends, the more he talked in class, and the more he talked in class, the lower his grades dipped.

Other issues began plaguing him as well. It was as if we were trapped in a vortex of troubles with no rescue in sight. A normally cheerful child, Josiah became increasingly discouraged. Nothing seemed to work—not even prayer. To Josiah, God would not—or could not—help him over this third-grade hump. By the middle of the second quarter, I was regularly reminding Josiah of our prayer that God "would please give us the best teacher for *him*."

"God doesn't make mistakes," I stressed, but the message didn't hit home.

Desperate to help, I created my version of encouragement cards. On each card—an 8" × 11" sheet of colored card stock—I typed an encouraging one-sentence prayer in the middle of the page. I included the related Scripture several lines down.

One card read, "Did you know kids can do great things for God?"

Another card noted, "I am Josiah, chosen by God for something really special."

And yet another card stated, "I am able to make a difference in the world."

All told, I created about a dozen and invited Josiah to choose his favorites to hang on his bedroom walls and place in his school binder. I wanted those messages to become visible reminders that God welcomed prayers from those who love Him, including school-aged children struggling to cope with issues beyond their control.

Despite my efforts, the situation escalated and a couple of his grades declined further. Frustrated, I sought prayer support from Carolyn, one of my closest friends. I originally met Carolyn, a dear lady more than a decade older than me, at my former church, where I was at that time an ordained minister. After many months of attending, Carolyn took the plunge and joined. She became a vital member of a church-sponsored weekly women's Bible study that I taught.

Despite our age difference, we quickly became friends, especially since we had many things in common, such as the fact that we were both single moms. Even when we both left our former church within months of each other and began to attend different churches, our friendship remained strong.

"Let me try talking to him," suggested Carolyn one evening after I shared Josiah's school problems with her. That night, she chatted briefly with Josiah and invited him to call her if he ever wanted to talk or pray.

Thus began an unlikely prayer partnership that lifted my son's spirits. As his grades went up, my anxiety went down. Several evenings a week, he would call Carolyn to tell her about his grades and any difficulty he had experienced during the school day. Over time, Josiah's in-class behavior improved, and his attitude skyrocketed.

After a short time, though, I noticed a pattern. Josiah would call Carolyn, share his information, request prayer, then hang up. "Why don't you ask her about her day," I mouthed one evening while he sat on my bed chatting away.

"Sister Carolyn," he began, "how was your day?" He looked at me, waiting for another prompt.

"Ask her if she needs prayer," I mouthed.

"Oh yeah," he said. "Do you need prayer?" He listened for a moment. "You do?" he asked with a surprised expression on his face. "Okay, I'll pray for you after you pray for me."

It was that simple. From then on, Josiah occasionally remembered to prompt Carolyn for her needs, after which he would pray accordingly. As he witnessed answered prayer, his faith surged. He started telling more people about the "power of prayer"—a phrase he picked up from Carolyn. It didn't matter if it was an adult or child, Christian or non-Christian. Once Josiah knew someone was discouraged because of illness or some other problem, he shared his story and offered to pray.

Family and friends drew strength from his prayers as they saw God answer Josiah's heartfelt petitions. Sharing their testimonies, they would often exclaim, "That boy can pray!" I'd chuckle, but quickly remind them that God deserved all the thanks. Nonetheless, every time I thought about how God worked through Josiah I wanted to shout for joy—

"Mommy, are you listening to me?" Josiah's insistent voice broke my reverie. His excited chatter about his first day concluded, he was ready for a snack—and his favorite cartoon.

Later that night, during our evening bedtime prayer, Josiah expressed gratitude for new classmates and a brightly decorated classroom. Taking a breath, he offered a few specific prayer requests. Finally, he concluded, "Thank you, God, for the very best teacher for *me*. I *really* had fun today."

~Lisa A. Crayton

About the Contributors

Sandi Banks and her husband, John, live in the Dallas, Texas, area. In addition to her role as wife, mom, and gramma to ten grandchildren, she enjoys music (harp, piano, guitar), language study, travel, Bible study, freelance writing, and speaking. Her Web site, *www.anchorsof hope.com*, offers hope and encouragement to women of all ages.

Alma Barkman of Winnipeg, Manitoba, Canada, is a freelance writer and photographer. She has had numerous articles and poems published, and she is the author of seven books. She is also a regular contributor to Daily Guideposts.

Cindy Boose lives in Columbia, South Carolina, where she keeps busy homeschooling her four teenage daughters, supporting Donald's Army career, and watching for other ways that God will use her.

Patricia Bridgman, author of *The Lord's Work*, is a retired public relations manager who now writes for children. Her articles have appeared in publications including *Highlights*, *Cricket*, and *Spiders*.

Connie Sturm Cameron is a freelance writer and has published dozens of inspirational articles. She is also the author of *God's Gentle Nudges* from Pleasant Word Publishers. Contact her at *www.conniecameron .com*; *conniec@netpluscom.com*; or P.O. Box 30, Glenford, OH 43739.

Ginny Caroleo is still happily married and lives in Hamden, Connecticut. She is involved in children's ministry at her church and works part-time as a childcare instructor for the public school district. However, her most fulfilling ministry is being the mother of her two teenage children.

Sandy Cathcart is a freelance writer living in the mountains of Oregon and often speaks and writes about her learning experiences with the Creator. Check out her blog at *www.sandycathcart.blogspot.com*

Dori Clark has been married to Duane for forty-five years. She is a mother of three and grandmother of eight. As a member of Oregon Christian Writers, she has written devotions for *God's Word for Today*, *A Cup of Comfort® Devotional for Mothers*, and *Word in Season*.

George Cop is retired and lives with his wife in Kansas. He faithfully encourages the men's ministry at his church and volunteers with Midwest Transplant Network. With his wife, he enjoys spending time at the lake in their RV.

Katherine J. Crawford is a freelance author whose work has been published in *A Cup of Comfort® for Mothers, Grace Givers, Soul Matters for Men, Soul Matters for Mothers,* and numerous magazines. She is the church news reporter for a weekly newspaper and she writes The Caregivers' Corner on *www.pmpawareness.org.*

Lisa A. Crayton is an award-winning freelance writer and the author of *I Want to Teach My Teens about Money Management.* Lisa A. Crayton (*www.LisaCrayton.com*) is mom to Josiah, who readily prays with and for his mom and others.

Virginia Dawkins has been published in *A Cup of Comfort® Devotional* and *A Cup of Comfort® for Christians.* She lives with her husband in Mississippi and writes inspirational articles for local newspapers. You may contact her at *jtdawk06@aol.com.*

Elsi Dodge is a single woman who travels across the continent in an RV, accompanied by her dog and cat. Retired after more than a quarter century of teaching special needs children, Dodge continues to tutor near Boulder, Colorado. She has completed both apprentice and journeyman courses through the Christian Writers Guild and attends Oregon and Colorado Christian Writers Conferences regularly. She can be contacted at *www.elsidodge.com.*

Kriss Erickson has been a freelance writer since 1975. She has had over 300 stories, book reviews, articles, recipes, and poems published. She holds a master of arts in counseling and a master's level Certificate of Spiritual Direction. She lives in Washington.

Anita Estes is an art teacher, dancer, and freelance writer who lives in upstate New York. She is honored in *Who's Who of American Teachers* for 2000 and 2005. Her writing appears in several publications, including *His Forever,* and she is the author of *When God Speaks.*

Mercedes B. Evans is a full-time writer of picture books for children and devotionals for adults. She spends many leisure hours boating with her husband and sharing her love of the Lord and her musical skills with her eight grandchildren.

Evangeline Beals Gardner is a stay-at-home mom, freelance writer, and piano teacher. She is very involved in compassion ministries, music, and worship arts at church. She makes specific time to talk, walk, dance, and be crazy with her two daughters. Her husband, dog, and two cats are amused observers to all the action.

Marion E. Gorman lives with her retired husband, Jim, in rural Pennsylvania. They have six children and nineteen grandchildren. She has been published in Mature Years, Seek, Penned From the Heart, Forever His, and she publishes her church newsletter. She seeks to share the profound way the Lord has worked in her life to encourage others.

Renee Gray-Wilburn provides freelance writing and editorial services for numerous publishers and ministries. She makes her home in Colorado Springs with her husband and three children. She enjoys the outdoors and spending time with her kids reading and doing crafts.

Albert Haley has had stories published in *The Atlantic*, *The New Yorker*, and *Rolling Stone*. He is also the author of *Home Ground: Stories of Two Families and the Land* (1979) and the novel *Exotic*, winner of the John Irving First Novel Prize (1982). Today he serves as writer-in-residence and Associate Professor of English at Abilene Christian University, in Abilene, Texas, where he lives with his wife, Joyce, and son, Coleman.

Clement Hanson is a retired Army physician and practices occupational medicine with Health One in Denver, Colorado. His wife, Mary, is a student at Denver Seminary. They are active members of Montview Boulevard Presbyterian Church. You can contact them at *hanson139@comcast.net*.

Jane Heitman is the author of hundreds of devotions and articles for Christian publications. She has also written books and articles in the education field. Her work has appeared in *Cup of Comfort® Devotional for Women* and *Cup of Comfort® Devotional for Mothers*. She works as a library technician in Colorado.

Sonja Herbert is the mother of six living children and the author of several award-winning stories. Her biographical novel, *Tightrope!* about her mother hiding in a circus during the Holocaust, recently won the distinguished Eaton Literary Award for best book of 2006. The story of her conversion to Christ is published in *His Forever*. Originally a native from Germany, she now lives in Hillsboro, Oregon.

Betty Jane Hewitt is a journalist and newspaper columnist who has been writing devotions, inspirational articles, and essays for over thirty years. She has had daily devotionals published in *The Quiet*

Hour, These Days, A Cup of Comfort® for Women, Penned from the Heart, and other Christian publications.

Stan Higley is a retired engineer. He resides in Fairport, New York, along the banks of the historic Erie Canal, where he writes fiction, creative nonfiction, poetry, and humor.

Jennie Hilligus lives in the Kansas City area and has been married for twenty-seven years. She was a freelance artist for Hallmark for nearly fourteen years. She enjoys spending time boating with her best friend/husband, and they love riding their Gold Wings. They have two adult children and a newly acquired son-in-law.

Linda Darby Hughes is a freelance writer and editor in Douglasville, Georgia. She began writing for publication at the advanced age of fifty-one, and her work has since appeared in numerous magazines, newspapers, and anthologies. Now she wishes she'd started sooner. Contact Linda at *dathasgirl@comcast.net.*

Sally Jadlow is the author of *The Late Sooner,* a work of historical fiction. She is also an award-winning author of poetry and short stories, a teacher of creative writing, a chaplain to corporations, wife, mother, and grandmother.

Jewell Johnson lives in Arizona with her husband, LeRoy. They are parents to six adult children and eight grandchildren. Besides writing, Jewell enjoys walking, reading, and quilting.

Helene C. Kuoni enjoys writing Christian devotions and short stories. She and her husband, John, recently coauthored a book: *Her Pen for His Glory: The 1860s Verse of Isabella Stiles Mead.* To relax, they escape to their summer home in Lake Pleasant, New York.

Sandra McGarrity lives and writes in Chesapeake, Virginia. Her writing has appeared in many magazines, anthologies, and books. She is the author of three novels: *Woody, Caller's Spring,* and *Virginia.* Visit her Web page at *hometown.aol.com/mygr8m8/myhomepage/books.html.*

Paula Moldenhauer is passionate about God's grace and freedom in Christ. She lives in Colorado, where she homeschools her four children, loves her husband, and writes her stories. Her Web site, *www.soulscents.us,* offers book reviews, parenting resources, and a free weekly devotional delivered to your e-mail box.

Karen Morerod is a pastor's wife, mother, and freelance writer. She is active in the prayer ministries and church groups.

Paula Munier has worked in publishing as a writer and editor for nearly twenty years. The mother of three lives in southern Massachusetts with her family, two dogs, and a cat.

Rod Nichols is the founder of For the Lord Ministries (*www.4theLord .com*), a traveling, teaching ministry. He is a pastor, teacher, and author of numerous books, including *God's Prosperity Plan* and *Walking with God*. For more on Rod's writing, visit *www.RodNichols.com*.

Donna Surgenor Reames lives on a horse farm in Pine Mountain, Georgia, with her family, including her three rambunctious daughters: Zoe, 13; Chloe, 10; and Caroline, 7. Donna worked as an R.N. for over twenty years before settling into life as a stay-at-home mom. She homeschools her oldest daughter and is working on a children's book.

Mary Catherine Rogers is an award-winning freelance writer from Georgia. She and her husband are the parents of three adult children and one spoiled Yorkshire terrier. She authors a monthly newspaper column titled *Cat-Tales*.

Debra Rose teaches college English and is the author of two books: *Shakespeare's World* and *Behind the Veil: An American Woman's Memoir of the 1979 Iran Hostage Crisis*. She also has published articles in Christian magazines such as *Marriage Partnership*, *Evangel*, and *On Mission*.

Using her own kids as inspiration, **Lori Z. Scott** has written numerous devotions, poems, short stories, and essays for children, teenagers, and mothers. She is the author of the Meghan Rose series, a line of children's fiction books to be released in fall 2007.

Yvonne Curry Smallwood believes in the power of prayer and credits her heavenly Father for the success He has afforded her as an author of several stories, articles, and one book.

Connie R. Smith is the proud mother of five children and grandmother of twelve. She lives in a small west Tennessee town where she thinks life is wonderful. She loves writing and had a story published in another *Cup of Comfort*® book.

Evelyn Rhodes Smith and her husband, Ted, live in Charleston, West Virginia, where they are active in Bible Center Church. Ted is a retired chemical engineer, and Evelyn is a writer who has been published in numerous magazines and books. They celebrated their fifty-seventh wedding anniversary on March 3, 2007.

Penny Smith resides in Pennsylvania, and has two sons and five grandchildren. She is a freelance writer and speaker and has been engaged in a preaching-teaching ministry, both at home and abroad. She is the author of *Gateways to Growth and Maturity*.

Gay Sorensen belongs to Calvary Chapel in Olympia, Washington, where she writes a monthly column for their newsletter. She also belongs to Sound View Christian Writers. Her poems, articles, and stories have appeared in several publications. She has three children, five grandchildren, four great grandchildren, and one sweet calico cat. All inspire her writings.

Rhonda Wheeler Stock is a professional writer and speaker who also teaches junior high special education. Her work has appeared in publications such as Focus on the Family's *Clubhouse*, *Moody* magazine, and *Herald of Holiness*. Rhonda and her husband live in a Kansas City suburb with their two teenagers.

Karen Strand's articles and poems have appeared in a wide variety of publications, including *Focus on the Family*, *Moody* magazine, *Today's Christian Woman*, and *Decision*, among others. She is the author of *Escape from the Fowler's Snare* and has contributed to nine gift/devotional books. Visit *www.karenstrand.com*.

Ronica Stromberg is the author of a picture book published by Lion-Hudson, England's largest independent publisher, and of four young adult titles published by Royal Fireworks Press here in the United States. Her stories appear regularly in Christian children's magazines such as Focus on the Family's *Clubhouse*.

Dianne Meredith Vogel lives in Michigan with her husband and one little dog. The three of them enjoy canoeing. Her work has appeared in three other *Cup of Comfort*® anthologies. She is currently working on a historical novel and a children's allegory.

Christine P. Wang is a freelance writer and assistant editor for two trade magazines. She has been published in *A Cup of Comfort*® *for Christians* and is currently writing her memoirs. Contact her at *cpw25@cornell.edu*.

Elisa Yager is a mom of two great kids. When she's not writing, she is a full-time Manager of Human Resources and Safety for a manufacturing firm. She has contributed to several *Cup of Comfort*® projects and resides in Hunterdon County, New Jersey.

Tell Your Story in the Next *Cup of Comfort*®

Welcome you have enjoyed *A Cup of Comfort*® *Book of Prayer* and that you will share it will all the special people in your life.

You won't want to miss our next heartwarming volumes, *A Cup of Comfort*® *for Single Mothers*, *A Cup of Comfort*® *for Horse Lovers*, and *A Cup of Comfort*® *for Cat Lovers*. Look for these new books in your favorite bookstores soon!

We're brewing up lots of other *Cup of Comfort*® books, each filled to the brim with true stories that will touch your heart and soothe your soul. The inspiring tales included in these collections are written by everyday men and women, and we would love to include one of your stories in an upcoming edition of *A Cup of Comfort*®.

Do you have a powerful story about an experience that dramatically changed or enhanced your life?

A compelling story that can stir our emotions, make us think, and bring us hope? An inspiring story that reveals lessons of humility within a vividly told tale? Tell us your story!

Each *Cup of Comfort*® contributor will receive a monetary fee, author credit, and a complimentary copy of the book. Just e-mail your submission of 1,000 to 2,000 words (one story per e-mail; no attachments, please) to *cupofcomfort@adamsmedia.com*. Or, if e-mail is unavailable to you, send it to:

A Cup of Comfort
Adams Media
57 Littlefield Street
Avon, MA 02322

You can submit as many stories as you'd like, for whichever volumes you'd like. Make sure to include your name, address, and other contact information and indicate for which volume you'd like to be considered. We also welcome your suggestions or stories for new *Cup of Comfort*® themes.

For more information, please visit our Web site: *www.cupofcomfort.com.*

We look forward to sharing many more soothing *Cups of Comfort*® with you!

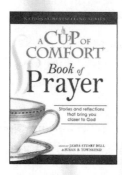